The Library of
Henry James

Studies in Modern Literature, No. 90

A. Walton Litz, General Series Editor

Professor of English
Princeton University

Consulting Editor:
Daniel Mark Fogel

Professor of English
Louisiana State University
Editor, *Henry James Review*

Other Titles in This Series

The Library of Henry James

Compiled and edited with essays by
Leon Edel and Adeline R. Tintner

U·M·I Research Press

Ann Arbor / London

Copyright © 1987
Leon Edel
Adeline R. Tintner

Produced and distributed by
UMI Research Press
an imprint of
University Microfilms Inc.
Ann Arbor, Michigan 48106

Library of Congress Cataloging in Publication Data

Edel, Leon, 1907–
   The library of Henry James.

   (Studies in modern literature ; no. 90)
   1. James, Henry, 1843–1916—Library—Catalogs.
2. James, Henry, 1843–1916—Books and reading. 3. Books
and reading in literature. I. Tintner, Adeline R.,
1912–   . II. Title. III. Series.
Z997.J32E33 1987   017'.6   87-24371
ISBN 0-8357-1856-5 (alk. paper)

British Library CIP data is available.

Contents

Figures

Acknowledgments

We are deeply indebted to Professor Daniel Mark Fogel not only for his list of the books in Lamb House, but for the complete supervision of the computerizing of the library list. Without his cooperation and facilitation of a vast project this list could never have been made. We are indebted to Sir Brian and Lady Batsford, the present residents of Lamb House, the late John James, Mr. Michael James and Dr. Roberta A. Sheehan. In addition to the staffs of the Houghton Library, the Bancroft Library and the C. Waller Barrett Collection (with special thanks to Joan Crane), we wish to thank a number of individuals who have found books which James owned. They include Leonard Granby, Paulette Greene, David Holmes, Kevin MacDonnell, John Maggs, Maurice F. Neville, Leona Rostenberg, Barry Scott, Madeleine B. Stern and Alexander D. Wainwright. We wish to thank also Hanna M. Bercovitch, Professors Jean Frantz Blackall, Harry Levin and Stanley Wertheim, as well as Mark Samuels Lasner for the bibliographic details concerning the books from James's library in their possession.

Lamb House, Entrance Hall
(Photograph by Alvin Langdon Coburn; collection Leon Edel)

The Two Libraries of Henry James

Leon Edel

When Henry James was a small boy his father described him as "a devourer of libraries." His generous family kept the child supplied with reading matter by presenting books on all occasions and by subscribing to the weeklies and monthlies with their serialized novels and melodramas. He describes in *A Small Boy and Others* being taken by his father to a bookstore and "the English smell" of the books. The pages of his memoirs are filled with old titles of novels long forgotten, from *The Lamplighter* to *The Initials*. In Europe there were books on all sides: and James remembered Merridew's English Library in Boulogne as the "solace of my vacuous hours and temple, in its degree too, of deep initiations." Here he got a large dose of Thackeray and the three-decker novels of the time. At maturity, he purchased whatever attracted his interest not only in England but in France and Italy: the lemon-covered French novels, their pages unopened, and an ivory paper knife inserted ready for its services, turns up in his writings; or the variously colored Italian works he read in the original. He was a regular buyer of books during his long working life—not a collector who looks for rarities and specialities but simply a highly informed reader, a "professional" who somehow sniffed out certain interests in volumes as soon as he glanced at them. Over the years he acquired many French classics as well as crowded shelves full of memoirs both English and French. He couldn't have enough autobiographies of the First Empire, the Napoleonic time—especially those of the military. Editions of the English classics, standard works of the poets and novelists, were available in the libraries. Certain writers were needed in his home so that he could readily reach for them. With the coming of fame, publishers sent him books, as did authors—including for example the eminent T. H. Huxley who sent a complete set of his scientific writings, for he was charmed by James.

A condensed version of this essay appeared in the University of Chicago Library Society *Bulletin* 3, no. 1 (Winter 1978).

Review copies also survived on James's shelves with pencilled-in notes from which he wrote his reviews.

His book-accumulations of the decades contain in this way hundreds of informal little messages written to himself—and now become messages to us. Important for posterity is the way in which James used his books. They were auxiliary to his writing; and this gave them importance above the autograph content which delights collectors. A line drawn down a page, a single word and page number, set down in the front of a book, a tiny cross at the beginning of a paragraph to enable him to find the place when he wanted it—an entire signal system exists in his library. In one volume there can be found the schema for a novel he wrote shortly after making this primitive outline. In my life of James I speak of these volumes—especially when they have a place, a date, a name—as "silent witnesses." Or we come on a Hawthorne novel (as I did once) which has on the title page Hawthorne's signature. Under this, Henry James signs his name. The two great American novelists of their time, the older and the younger, here keep eternal company. Perhaps the special message to posterity had been willed by at least one of the parties.

Henry James's executor, his nephew (named for Henry James Sr.) paused in 1916, after his uncle's death, to reflect on the disposal of the volumes in the glassed-in cases in Lamb House. They were in every room and crammed also into a series of shelves on the top floor, the servants' quarters. Many of the books were in rare bindings, for James liked a handsome book and good print; a well-laid-out page thrilled him, as it does certain writers. His own New York Edition, for which he laid down the terms, has a great deal of white space around the handsome typography and the quality of the original paper used in the first printing is enhanced by a watermark using his monogram. Henry James III, heir to Lamb House and its contents, regarded the books simply as books. It seems never to have occurred to him that they were as intimately a part of James's creation as his notebooks. In a letter to his brother Bill, the painter, he pondered whether he should sell the library or parcel it out to the family. A "foundation executive" who had worked for the Rockefeller and Carnegie, his training had been in law, not in letters, even though he later won the Pulitzer Prize for a biography of Charles W. Eliot of Harvard. He recognized that the first editions had value; he was concerned about the safety of the books if Lamb House were rented—even to remarking that James's sets would suffer if a single volume in a set were damaged. The French memoirs struck him as out-of-date; the English books from 1860 on he felt were of interest only to historians of the period.

By the end of the first war he reached a solution. Henry III removed to his home in New York some of the choice first editions, a number of the American writers and books of American interest as well as valued autograph copies, such as James's Stevensons and Kiplings. A goodly number of books, especially those dealing with painters, and old family books, were placed later in 95 Irving Street—

William James's house in Cambridge—where Billy James and his wife, the former Alice Runnells, would live for many years. Some books were in the possession of Peggy, James's niece, and a few volumes made their way to Dublin, New Hampshire, the home of the youngest son, Alexander James, also a painter, and his wife Frederika.

Henry III left in Lamb House about 4,000 books, many quite as important as those he removed. An ideal tenant was found in E. F. Benson, a son of the former Archbishop of Canterbury and a skillful writer of light fiction who wrote the amusing "Lucia" and "Mapp" books about life in Rye. Benson had known Henry James and accommodated himself readily to the fine old house. He was still living there in 1937 when I wrote and asked whether I might spend an afternoon in the house and inspect the books. Benson responded promptly and cordially. He would be away on the day I planned to come, but the servants would take care of me. However, when I got off the train at Rye and asked my way to Lamb House I was told that the man on the platform across the way was Mr. Benson. We had enough time before his train left to talk of the books which he said remained in the original book cases; his own books had been relegated to one wall in the Garden Room—"the housekeeper has instructions to show you." I climbed the hill and for the first time crossed the threshold into an important part of Henry James's past.

I

Let me try to recall James's library in its original setting. I refresh my memory of some parts of it from the inventory I obtained some years later. There were books in the Green Room upstairs, where I knew James worked in the evenings and on cold days in winter. The books were strangely miscellaneous, as if gathered from other shelves, consulted and left mixed up with those tenanted here. There was a first edition of Hawthorne's *Transformation*—the English edition of *The Marble Faun* to which James often alluded, a novel distinctly related to *Roderick Hudson.* He had the edition of 1860 in three volumes. Then there was George Borrow's *Celebrated Trials,* the works of Gray in three volumes, the works of Washington Irving, and the novels of Constance Fenimore Woolson, the American regional novelist who had been a close friend of James's during the last decade of her life. James had her personal copies of her works. He also had some volumes of Browning duplicated elsewhere and Tennyson's, and incongruously, in the midst of these books, copies of five of Hugh Walpole's novels, inscribed. He had a volume of Edward Fitzgerald's letters, books by the French critic Paul de Saint-Victor, several George Sand novels, President De Brosses' *Lettres familières,* a volume of Diderot, Marie Bashkirtseff's journal, Dante in a Florentine edition of 1874 in vellum gilt, some of D'Annunzio's novels in Italian (annotated by him for his late essay on that novelist), and a number of Italian volumes purchased, as we can see from his datings, during his first journey to Italy in 1869. In his earlier years James often dated books on acquisition and sometimes, years later, he overlooked the old signatures and dates, and signed the book a second time.

In a miniature bookcase I saw the works of Paul Bourget, mostly presentation copies. Here also I found some volumes of Heine, which had been owned by James's father, who signed his name as if the J were printed, while his son always brought the J below the line. If one doesn't note this distinction, it is easy to take the father's signature for that of his son.

In a bookcase near the door of the Green Room James had a goodly number of French books including many volumes of Renan; some of these had also belonged to his father. There was a copy of *Les Fleurs du mal* in an edition of 1872, that is about the time of James's essay on Baudelaire; twenty-three volumes of Taine, bound in half-mottled gilt calf and some in half-crushed morocco; a good many volumes of memoirs of the post-Revolutionary period in France and in particular the Empire; the memoirs of Casanova in ten volumes, half yellow calf; Flaubert's *Bouvard et Pécuchet* and the *Trois contes;* and the novels of Gyp to which he alludes in his preface to *The Awkward Age.* Clearly James arranged his books casually. Yet I suspect he knew where each volume was.

I have offered these titles to suggest the kind of library he had; it was heterogeneous and comparatively modern. Let us now stroll into the charming panelled little Oak Room on the ground floor, leading to the garden. Here you might have seen all of the works of John Addington Symonds, about whom James wrote a short story called ''The Author of 'Beltraffio' '' (although he denied Symonds was the original of his fictional author). Here he had also some Gissing and a significant series of Napoleonic memoirs bound in half red morocco including Marbot, Marshal Macdonald, the Count de Chaptal, Bigarré, Masson, and Lévy. They later came into my possession and I have described them in my life of James. His complete Flaubert was here in eight volumes in half red morocco, also the *Arabian Nights* and the illustrated *Contes drolatiques* of Balzac which I consider myself fortunate to own. Then, in a secrétaire-bookcase, a large number of his friend Edmund Gosse's books, some autographed Kiplings, a volume of Tennyson given him by his father which he had owned since boyhood, and the writings of the Goncourts. On one table in a miniature bookcase, he had Browning's *Men and Women* in the two-volume first edition, yellow calf by Bedford, and the four volumes of the *Ring and the Book* bound by Rivière. We know how carefully these were read.

The Garden Room held my attention, a detached room where in good weather James walked up and down on a plain carpet (no figure in it) and dictated to his various typists. All of his late novels were written in this way. Here he had the several volumes of Madame Karénine's life of George Sand, which years later I found in a pile of books on the floor of a London bookshop and which James used in writing some of the six articles he devoted to the great feminist. Here also was his Toqueville, which I ultimately owned, and the Constance Garnett translations of the works of his beloved friend Ivan Turgenev; and he had also some French translations of Turgenev that had belonged to Miss Woolson as well as the Turgenevs inscribed to himself. Years later, I came across one of these on a general circulation shelf in Harvard's Widener Library, and reported its presence to the librarian of the Houghton, where all the rarities belong. I need not add that it was transferred promptly to its proper place. Mysterious are the wanderings of a famous man's books.

In the Garden Room the novelist had the complete Browning, and the complete Kipling inscribed, various Ibsens, more French memoirs, books he had reviewed long ago with the kind of notes I have mentioned; there were inscribed Daudets, the Eversley Shakespeare of 1899, various Edith Whartons and in this company eight volumes of Milton, if I remember correctly, annotated by James, alongside the poet's life by Mitford. James also kept in the Garden Room H. G. Wells's novels which that novelist kept sending as they came out, all inscribed in the friendliest fashion with no hint of their future literary quarrel. Here too James kept the novels of his very old friend Howells.

In choosing at random these examples, I hope I am not creating an impression that Henry James's library was essentially *belles lettres*. This would not be altogether accurate. He had many volumes of history and philosophy, a great deal of Dr. Johnson, the diaries of Samuel Pepys, and so on. And once again we must remember that James for some forty years used the libraries at his clubs, which prided themselves on having not only current volumes but books accumulated earlier during their long history. And then James had available to him the London Library to which he belonged, and which Carlyle had angrily founded when he discovered, early in the century, that the British Museum's books could not be taken home.

Before I left Rye during that all-too-brief visit, I browsed in the local bookshop. Country bookstores can be full of surprises and this one had two such for me. The bookseller, learning of my interest, produced two volumes which had pasted in a label "From the Library of Henry James." The novelist's nephew had cleared some shelves at one time and sold them, with the label inserted. The volumes were French court memoirs and were bound in cloth. James had signed his name on the end papers. I bought them, I think, for a pound apiece, which wasn't considered cheap in 1937. So I had my souvenirs of that visit.

II

The library came into my life again more than ten years later. The second war had intervened. I gave little thought to Henry James during my time of service in General Patton's Third Army, though I did stumble on some James letters in Paris, which I entered on the day of the city's liberation, riding in a recon to the rear of a long procession, at the head of which rode General Charles de Gaulle. That, however, is another story. Shortly after the war's end, when I was in civilian clothes again in New York, Henry James III died. This brought me into touch with his widow, a plump plain matron, sister of Ruth Draper, the monologuist. Dorothea Draper had been married to a physician; widowed in middle life, she had married the divorced Harry James. I wrote a letter of condolence to Dorothea and she asked me to come and see her. The nephew had taken care of most James family details—he had given the James papers to Harvard and his widow inherited Lamb House. She found that I was one of the few people who could give her information about some matters relating to "Uncle Henry," as the relatives called him. Lamb House had been damaged by Nazi bombing and the Garden Room was destroyed. The books had been rescued and stored away by the local bookseller. Dorothea James was planning a trip to England and she asked me whom she might see and I gave her various names. I doubt whether she had ever read a line of Henry James. She was a good-natured, wealthy society woman who spent her days serving on hospital boards and assorted charities and being a loyal wife to the distinguished Henry James III.

We had a number of pleasant Sunday lunches before she went abroad armed with her widowship and her organizing zeal. One day before she left she found a folder relating to me, and I could read all my old letters, and the very correct way in which Harry James had ascertained my qualifications to edit James's plays. On another day she found a folder relating to Lamb House and this too she presented to me. She showed me the several hundred volumes of the James library Harry had brought to New York in 1931, some at the flat on the Upper East Side and many in their house on Long Island where I spent a few fascinating bookish weekends. Fascinating because it does give one a start (as I have described) to pull down a copy of Hawthorne signed both by Hawthorne and James. Dorothea gave me James's Toqueville, the four volumes bound by James as two. I quickly learned that I could not tell her of my finds on her shelves—for she very promptly used to sell the volumes to booksellers. She said Harry had told her to dispose of whatever James books she did not want and give the money to his young nephews. When I hinted that I would be glad to purchase some from her, she said she couldn't do that: she was willing to present books to me but not to sell—and since she was anxious to sell and did so impulsively, she gave me a few gifts for which I was grateful. It was clear to me, at any rate, that when Dorothea set off for England in that now-distant post-war world, when you still flew by propeller plane, and when England was still gladly receiving "Bundles for Britain," that she did not place great store in the books. I had hoped for the library's preservation. She had uses for such revenue as it would bring.

I will add a non-bookish postscript to this. Dorothea put all her husband's clothes into various Bundles for Britain and they were shipped to England. He had elegant clothes and in each was sewn his name, Henry James. Years later, the poet laureate, John Betjeman, used to proclaim with pride that he was wearing novelist Henry James's underwear and his waistcoats. He was photographed for the magazines in one of these waistcoats. The members of the James family never disillusioned him. He was wearing the nephew's, of course, not the novelist's. But for him there was only one Henry James—and wasn't that the name on the label?

<h2 style="text-align:center">III</h2>

Dorothea James telephoned me the day she returned from London. Her trip had been a triumph. "Do come to lunch Sunday—I have so much to tell you." I came full of curiosity and misgivings. It was pleasant to learn that everyone had made a great fuss over her because her name was James. I had sent her to Theodora Bosanquet, Henry James's remarkable typist—the last of the line and the most brilliant—who was by now literary editor of the feminist journal *Time and Tide*. She had put Dorothea in touch with others. Henry III had spoken of her to me as if she were simply one of his uncle's servants; and Mrs. James had felt that she had taken too many liberties when James had his first stroke and there was no "family" present to take responsibility for the running of his household when he was wholly in the hands of doctors, his mind dulled and wandering. Actually the evidence showed that Miss Bosanquet did what any competent secretary would do at such a moment; she made such decisions as were absolutely necessary, until Mrs. William crossed the submarine-infested Atlantic to be at the novelist's bedside.

Dorothea's important news was that she had presented Lamb House to the British nation, to the National Trust, as symbol of the enduring friendship between the United States and the United Kingdom. I would help her in due course to draw up the wording for the statement of gift which hangs in the memorial room. It memorializes Henry James and the generosity of the nephew and his widow. I later found that the other nephews were not altogether happy at Dorothy's initiative; they would have preferred to deep Lamb House in the family. But she had the last word.

I listened to her enthusiastic recital. She was astonished—as Mrs. William James had been—that Henry James's name had so much magic in England. The children of William James had picked up the curious disparagement of the novelist by his elder brother, who in a famous letter characterized him as his "younger, shallower and vainer brother." Some have argued this was a mere jest—but is so it was a very strange jest, as most persons who read the documents agree.

I said to Dorothea as she handed me my plate with the Sunday roast:

"And the Library . . . ?"

"The Library?"

"Yes, Henry James's books, the ones at Lamb House that were stored by Fabes after the Garden House was bombed."

"Oh those! I sold them." And then, pleased at having driven what she thought was a good bargain, "Fabes gave me £200 for them." One thousand dollars for some 4,000 books, many signed by James or his author friends, or association volumes, all related to the novelist's work. Many libraries in the United States would have paid many thousands more and included the packing and shipping.

I must have coughed or moved nervously for she said, "Mr. Edel, did I do anything wrong?"

I said, "Those are all very valuable books, and your husband had removed only a certain part of them."

She squirmed, I think, but said, "Well, Fabes had taken good care of them; and I couldn't see myself bringing them back with me."

Her action and remarks reflected, as we can see, her late husband's attitude toward the books of his uncle.

I said, "It would be useful if some record existed of the books. Did your husband ever have the library inventoried?"

"Oh yes," she said. "Harry had one made long ago. I know where it is. I'll get it for you right away." She came bustling back, very pleased to have put her hand instantly on what I asked for. "You may keep it," she said. "I have no further use of it."

I do not want to suggest this as a literal report of our talk during this strange moment, when she was so elated by her English journey and I was unable to join in her feelings. It was approximately the way our conversation ran.

Typed on the front page of the inventory were the words "Catalogue of the Library of the late Henry James at Lamb House, Rye, Sussex." And in Henry III's handwriting there was the following: "I took Hodgson's copy of the catalogue he made, struck out books sold or brought home in 1931, noted transfers from one room and book case to another." He added he had then had the list clean-typed from his copy. This was the list I now had. The list we give in this volume takes into account every book that was in Lamb House after the 1931 changes, as well as those dispersed. What remained was still, as I have said, a very substantial and important library, indeed unique of its kind, as if tailored to the master. Mrs. James soon discovered the meaning of my words, for shortly afterwards it was decided to have some books from the library in the memorial room. She then had to buy some back and discovered how much Fabes was charging for them. Today his prices seem very moderate compared to their present value in the marketplace.

Possession of the inventory enabled me to write to Fabes, who owned the bookshop in Rye, and to purchase from him some of the less expensive volumes that meant so much to me for the writing of Henry James's life. Indeed some of the books I valued most—like those that had belonged to Miss Woolson—had little value for the bookseller who, after all, could not know her place in the biography. His high prices were marked on the bindings, and when I bought

James's Napoleonic collection I paid for these rather than the novelist's pencil marks in the books which I prized. My negotiations with Fabes were enlivened by his love of American bacon and various other delicacies during the continuing post-war British rationing. We did a lot of bartering, for I sent him a goodly number of food parcels.

It was frustrating to think how many books had been kept together all those years and how widely certain components of the library were scattered. With the few volumes I bought before the bookseller issued his catalogues, and some I acquired later from members of the James family, I started my own little collection. I would keep intact one tiny corner of Lamb House. This I did. It was a corner that had special importance for me and when I stopped collecting I had four hundred volumes, including some that John James presented to me from the collection in Irving Street. I chose copies which had Jamesian markings; I remained faithful to my quest for "silent witnesses." On one occasion, I told William Jackson, the librarian of the Houghton Library, of Dorothea James's tendency to sell James library volumes from her shelves whenever she heard of something of value, and that enterprising diplomat of the book world in very short order charmed her into promising to leave all the remainder of Henry James III's books to Harvard. Indeed, after her death, I spent a long afternoon with Jackson helping him find on the shelves of Dorothea's Long Island house the Lamb House volumes. (My own collection later went to the University of Virginia. I did not want to bring it to Hawaii, where I would have to provide those conditions of temperature and protection against real bookworms and other book-consuming organisms and where mildew and damp make book collecting a considerable hazard.)

IV

Since booklovers have the fun of finding and assembling books of writers who have passed from the human scene but who have left themselves planted in folios, quartos, octavos and now in universal paperbacks, let us invent a special collector, one filled with zeal and love of letters who is also an admirer of the American novelist, Henry James. Let us say he decides to collect every book mentioned or hinted at in Henry James's twenty novels and his 112 tales—in other words, the books listed by Adeline Tintner in her valuable inventory-essay at the end of this volume. Let us draw a line between these and the obvious books—the books James reviewed and criticized and analyzed in his non-fictional writings. A collector of paintings does not have the same opportunity. There are quite as many paintings as books mentioned in James's fiction, but these happen to be among the finest the world has known and they are distributed in museums along the beaten path of James's travels from London to Italy. It would take a lot of hijacking to form that collection. In practical terms, it is the book collector who can assemble a second library of Henry James. If he were to ask where he should start, I would say "The Story of a Year," James's first signed tale, published in the *Atlantic Monthly* just as the Civil War was ending in the spring of 1865.

The characters in this story are named Robertson, Robert, James, Elizabeth, John, all James family names. The Robert is Robert Bruce and he has a sister named Jane. And the heroine of the story of life behind the lines has read a particular book, *Scottish Chiefs* by Jane Porter, and Bruce is referred to as her "Scottish Chief." Here is one of the first books we must put on the shelf of James's second library, that romantic novel of old childhoods and past generations, then to be found in almost every home. A little thought suggests to us what would become characteristic of James's literary method as Tintner defines it. James is invoking for us the bloody civil wars of Scotland as a parallel to America's Civil War; and the reading about these wars rather than the participation in them, for he did not fight in the Civil War. In fact he made a point of saying in the story that the records of wars can be read in history books and newspapers, but the record he is writing is that of the reverse of the tapestry—the home scene, the sweethearts waiting for their warring lovers, the widows left alone with the memory of their dead.

There we have then, in James's acknowledged first story, a suggestion of his way of making his own fiction a criticism of fiction, and of embodying the literary past of the race as painters embody on their canvases the work of their predecessors. The first example is almost too simple when we compare it with the late James method. Who hasn't wondered, for example, about those few words exchanged between Maria Gostrey and Lewis Lambert Strether in the opening scenes of *The Ambassadors*. Miss Gostrey gives Strether her card, and she confesses she has looked up Strether's name in the hotel register.

"I like your name," she says to him. "Mr. Lewis Lambert Strether—particularly the Lewis Lambert. It's the name of a novel of Balzac's."

"Oh, I know that!" said Strether.

"But the novel's an awfully bad one."

"I know that too," Strether smiled.

Our mythical collector coming on this knows that he must find an edition of *Louis Lambert*. He may wonder whether to acquire it in English or in French. Our answer is that it would have to be in French, but the collector may have to acquire the entire *Comédie humaine* of Balzac in its original 23-volume edition, for it was probably here that James first read *Louis Lambert,* unless he had had some still earlier edition. It would be safe to acquire that many-volumed edition because the collector would soon discover that James is constantly using Balzac; in fact there are probably more allusions to Balzac novels than to most other works, allusions direct and indirect. As to why James plants *Louis Lambert,* one of Balzac's philosophical novels, so early in *The Ambassadors* we can only conjecture. If he announces it is a bad novel, we are safe to assume he plans to improve on it. It is a novel about an education, and Strether is about to undergo a middle-aged education in Europe. He will dwell on the difference between the *mores* of Woollett, Massachusetts and those of Paris. If we read *Louis Lambert,* we would also find much discussion of a treatise on the will—a subject which was the deep concern of Henry's brother William. And in *The Ambassadors,* we find ourselves in the midst of a discussion of free will and determinism in which Strether propounds Henry James's philosophy: that man can live best by cultivating an "illusion of freedom," even though he is a creature of conditioning. It is clear that as James advanced in life his literary allusions—the books he scattered in the pages of his own writings—came to have profound meanings as works not only of reference and criticism but as a subtle anagogical device, as Miss Tintner has demonstrated in her recent volume *The Book World of Henry James: Appropriating the Classics.* This was the response of a writer to a vision of a past which seems to say to all artists that everything has been tried, that here are the millions of books already written, and what is the artist to do who wants to add to their number? The greatest artists have understood that the best thing they can do is to renovate old forms by creating new ones, *using* the past rather than relinquishing it. Ezra Pound was doing this when he turned to Provençal poetry or rewrote Propertius. T. S. Eliot did it by grafting lines out of classic poetry into his own, representing a continuity of thought and allusion, a feeling of profound kinship, a peculiar personal intimacy with a dead author—as when Eliot made poems out of Lancelot Andrewes' old sermons.

So Henry James, before these moderns, took old stories and rewrote them very much as Manet repainted a Raphael classic in *Le Déjeuner sur l'Herbe.* Out of the library in James's stories the novelist made new books that have endeared themselves to us, and that reflect the America of his time and more profoundly still the dilemma in which Americans found themselves in the nineteenth century. They had been fashioned in a new land, divorced and even washed clean of the culture of the old, and many had to learn all over again what the old countries had learned long ago. I have had occasion to suggest that Ezra Pound's "make it new" can be read as a cry of desperation. To make new worlds we must use old worlds. Even writers of science fiction are hard put to fashion humans on other planets who do not have some part of our own shapes. Man cannot imagine himself in any other image than his own, although he may give himself more legs or arms, or change the contours of his body, or imitate the animals as in science fiction. He works with the given shape—or if you will, from the godly image.

When we tell ourselves this, we can enter into the fascinating literary game of association and terminology, of criticism and emulation, which James played in his novels and tales. In this game he tells himself that Hawthorne came out of a primitive America; a later arrival, like himself, could redo Hawthorne benefitting by the accretions of time and civilization. Thus *The Marble Faun,* a novel which reflects the complexity of Puritanism but views Rome with simplicity; in

James it becomes *Roderick Hudson,* in which the complexity of Rome is shown in its effect upon the grandchildren of the puritans. I like Adeline Tintner's demonstration some years ago of the way in which Henry James introduces the false romanticism of *Madame Bovary* into the false romantic of the heroine of the *Portrait of a Lady* by an allusion to that masterpiece. In the *Portrait,* Isabel Archer says that her ideal of life is "a swift carriage of a dark night, rattling with four horses over roads that one can't see—that's my idea of happiness." This kind of wish for a blind destiny is attacked by Isabel's friend Henrietta, who says she is "acting like the heroine of an immoral novel." If we think upon the best known "immoral novel," Miss Tintner reminds us, we think of *Madame Bovary,* and we immediately remember Emma Bovary's romantic rides in carriages with her lovers. We establish the Jamesian connection when we come upon "au galop de quatre chevaux, elle était emportée depuis huit jours vers un pays nouveau." We can see the resemblance to the Jamesian passage—"with the gallop of four horses she had been, for eight days, carried toward a new country." This is what Isabel asked for. We are justified, I think, in adding *Madame Bovary* to the shelves of the second James library, more especially since we find the book also providing a picture of the convent education of James's American Madame de Mauves, in one of his early and very popular tales.

V

I cannot resist proposing another work for our imaginary collector. If we look into a little tale called "Glasses," we find James describing an Oxford aesthete: "He was supposed to be unspeakably clever; he was fond of London, fond of books, of intellectual society and of the idea of a political career. That such a man should be at the same time fond of Flora Saunt [the heroine of the story] attested, as the phrase in the first volume of Gibbon has it, the variety of his inclinations." Notice how precise James has been in specifying the relevant volume.

We add Gibbon to our hypothetical collection, or at least the first volume. Miss Tintner has located the precise reference in chapter 7 of *The Decline and Fall* in the description of the Roman Emperor Gordianus the Younger: "Twenty-two acknowledged concubines, and a library of sixty-two thousand volumes, *attested the variety of his inclinations.*" James is having his little joke in contrasting a licentious Roman emperor—but an emperor with a huge library—with an Oxford aesthete.

It may be valuable for us to remember that what happens in the story is that one master of irony invokes another. The heroine has wonderful eyes that prove "good for nothing but to roll about like sugar balls in a child's mouth" for she cannot use them. She refuses to wear glasses and becomes blind. As we read on we see that James is placing in this story, written at the moment of Pater's death, the question of Pater's aestheticism and his great success in concealing his life from the world. He was "the mask without the face." He had done everything with his pen, his style, his genius and not at all with his person. (He was the exact opposite of Hemingway who had done everything with his person.) The Jamesian imagination seems to be bringing Gibbonesque irony together with Paterian anonymity in his story of a woman whose quest for beauty gives her a mask for a face: her eyes are as blank as the eyes of a statue, through her false aestheticism. She has retained her facade; she has turned herself into a creature to be seen—but who cannot see. For James who believed that to see is to live—so great was his visuality—this is a form of death-in-life. I might add that in James's library the 1871 eight-volume edition of Gibbon's *The Decline and Fall* edited by Milman and Guizot occupied a prominent place.

There is still another game we might play with James and books. We might obtain from a publisher a series of dummies, that is bound books showing their external appearance but containing only blank pages. They too could be masks without faces. On these I would letter a series of titles to be found in Henry James's stories—books written by his characters that in reality exist only in James's imagination. There is "Beltraffio," whose author is hated by his wife for the things he writes. There is the factitious novel "Deep Down," by Gwendolyn Erme, in three volumes. There is Ralph Limbert's "The Major Key," or his other book "The Hidden Heart" and finally his unfinished novel "Derogation." There is Neil Paraday's fragment in "The Death of the Lion," which is irretrievably lost at a weekend party and which becomes posthumous and unnamed. There is a work called *Obsessions* by Guy Walsingham, who turns out to be a woman, and then Dora Forbes, who is a man, has written a work called "The Other Way Round."

Our mythical collector would have to study James's expertise in bindings as well, and to remember that there is a whole library of bound books in *The Princess Casamassima* because the young Keatsian hero is a little bookbinder out of the London slums. Miss Tintner has an entire section in her essay on this subject. In James's library his Browning, to which I have referred, was bound by the great binder Francis Bedford in yellow calf extra, gilt-edged, and he had also bound James's two volumes of Ford's dramatic works in calf extra. James's five volumes of Plato, translated by Jowett, were bound by Rivière, the French binder who lived in London, in polished calf extra, top-edged with gilt. There were many other fine bindings and this talk of books and bindings fills the pages of *The Princess*. And Tintner mentions the seventy volumes by Victor Hugo bound in red and gold which Lambert Strether, on the impulse of a moment, buys and later thinks about as he is sitting in Notre Dame—quite appropriately, since Hugo wrote *The Hunchback of Notre Dame*. We see how difficult it is to exhaust this subject once one is launched. What an unique library a collector could form and I have not touched on the many ephemeral volumes, the popular fiction, the minor works now forgotten, that would find their way into it. Henry James demonstrates in this use of literature and of the past—with a finesse perhaps unequalled in fiction—how literature comes out of literature, and how much it is nonsense to think of literature as coming exclusively out of life. If we could gather in one immense library all the works of the human imagination written since the beginning of writing, what we would have would be a vast record of human imaginings and overwhelming proof of our myth-creating powers. This record is a world composed entirely of language and it is the way in which we translate into language humanity's life-processes. We live, after all, largely in our minds, perceptions, feelings—and out of these create our dreams, fancies, visions, articulating scenes present to our eyes and scenes present in our memories, derived in turn from the memories and scenes of others. Northrop Frye and Joseph Campbell have demonstrated this to us in the fullness of their writings.

So the libraries of Henry James embody the realities of this world and the realities of what we imagine about this world; the books James found himself buying because of his love of books and print and fine bindings and the books that had been created by other imaginations which also exist though not necessarily on his shelves. They exist, however, in his books, quite as if they were on his shelves. What endless potential for fun and inspiration we can discover in the texts of James's writings and the subtle game of books that he conducts from volume to volume as he conducts it with all else that man created—the silver plate, the artifacts, the lace, the dresses, the architecture, the paintings, the "spoils" of war and of the hunt and of the collector and the museum, which encapsulate within them the history of civilization. When we understand this, we understand why James's final message to the world was embodied in a statement, "It is art that *makes* life, makes interest, makes importance . . . and I know of no substitute whatever for the force and beauty of its process."

Few artists have been brave enough to assert this kind of omnipotence: it requires a particular kind of courage to do so. They tend to say instead that life makes art—which is but half of the truth. For it is man's imagination of life that has made all the books we put on our shelves. That is the supreme lesson of Henry James's library and we may rejoice that in spite of its unfortunate dispersal the greater part of it has been preserved and is available to us in various repositories.

Henry James's Library:

Titles from the Original Inventory and Various Collections, Augmented from Other Sources

The problem we faced in compiling a list of the volumes known to have been dispersed from Henry James's library was essentially one of collation of diverse inventories and records. The list we are publishing is by no means complete; but it comprises in all probability the largest part of the library. There existed in the first instance the Hodgson inventory which Leon Edel obtained from Dorothea James. Subsequently there were the three catalogues issued by Gilbert H. Fabes, the bookseller at Rye, who took care of storage of the library during the second war. It was necessary to collate these with the Hodgson inventory and various holdings in U.S. libraries, which consisted of: a) the books Henry James III removed from Lamb House, which were in part acquired by the Houghton Library, although some of the volumes were sold earlier by Dorothea James; b) the library of some 400 volumes collected from the Lamb House sales and other sources by Leon Edel, which are now in the Barrett Collection of the University of Virginia together with volumes acquired by Mr. Barrett from booksellers; c) the Bancroft Library collection of volumes from James's library which were the property of Mrs. Bruce Porter (Peggy James); and d) the Viscount David Eccles' collection of 167 French volumes, now part of Adeline Tintner's collection. Some volumes are privately held and derive from 95 Irving Street, Cambridge, where William James, younger brother of Henry James 3rd, had a considerable number of Lamb House volumes and old James family books. We have only a partial list of these.

In addition we had to collate later collections and a number of odd volumes in other places, including the volumes displayed in bookcases in the memorial room in Lamb House.

These lists overlap and contain duplications. The three Fabes catalogues need to be briefly described. They were issued in three successive years, from 1949–1951, and constituted numbers 17–19 of the series Fabes issued from his bookshop during his lifetime. The 1949 catalogue lists the James books starting on page 41 under the heading "Books from the Library of Henry James, Removed from Lamb House,

Rye, comprising belles lettres, English and American Literature, Italian, Travel and other subjects. All signed by Henry James or being Presentation Copies to him." The list runs from page 41 to page 50, where a new heading, "London," is given. Here Fabes lists certain volumes James acquired when he planned to write a book about the London he knew. On page 51 another heading is "French Books." This runs to page 52 and continues onto the unpaginated back cover, inside and verso. All the James items are numbered from 942 to 1165.

The second catalogue, of 1950, contains a list of James's books under the title of "Association Items from the Library of Henry James" and runs from pages 7 to 10; and these items are numbered 126–190. The heading on page 7 reads "Association Items in English, French, and Italian from the Library of Henry James."

The 1951 catalogue, number 19, gives some miscellaneous James library books mixed in with books from other sources. These will be found in pages 8–11, the items numbered 168 to 246, each James item carefully designated.

It is known that Fabes's catalogues did not list all the books he sold. Some books were sold before the catalogues were issued, and a number sold back to Mrs. James, who wished to place them in the memorial room. There were also a number of books which James had not signed, including French paperbacks bound and unbound. These Fabes had at one time in a bookcase at the rear of his building; he sold them to various purchasers. And as we know, Fabes handled earlier batches of volumes sold him by Henry James III with a printed label identifying them as from the James library.

It is only during the last few years that lists of James's books now in the Houghton Library, the Bancroft Library and the C. Waller Barrett Collection have finally been completed and made available to researchers. And last autumn we added Daniel Fogel's inventory of the books now at Lamb House, made through the good offices of Sir Brian and Lady Batsford, the present tenants of the house; and we added our holdings, as well as the Fabes and Hodgson lists. We regularized the basic information about each book (author, title, city, publisher and date of publication), adding the symbol A if the book was signed by James. (He signed many books on acquiring them; and he signed many others later in Lamb House—we can tell the difference by the pens he used). This in our compilation is followed by a letter or letters indicating the location of the volume at the present time.

The next step was undertaken by Professor Fogel. Under his direction, Katharine Paine designed a program that allowed Patricia Gabilondo (then *Henry James Review* Fellow) to enter every title on the seven unalphabetized lists into the mainframe computer at Louisiana State University. The computer then sorted to create an alphabetical master list. We then deleted the duplications from the Fabes-Hodgson lists whenever the titles appeared in their present known locations. The next process was to insert accent marks and complete first names and to correct certain bibliographic errors arising from the vagaries of computers and errors of booksellers. Finally, the list published here is an enlarged, corrected version of our compilation of "The Library of Henry James," which was published under Professor Fogel's editorship in the *Henry James Review* 4, no. 3 (Spring 1983).

L.E.

A.R.T.

THE LIBRARY OF HENRY JAMES

The description of each book includes identifying sigla combining an A (signed by James) or 0 (not signed by James) with one of the locations keyed below. The several university collections have complete bibliographic details, including the number of volumes in each title, whether or not the pages have been cut, and what, if any, exact marginal notes appear. Transcripts of their lists are available from the libraries.

B	Hanna M. Bercovitch's Collection, New York, New York
BAN	The Bancroft Library, University of California, Berkeley, California
BAR	The C. Waller Barrett Collection, University of Virginia, Charlottesville, Virginia
BL	Jean Frantz Blackall's Collection, Ithaca, New York
CB	Carter Burden's Collection, New York, New York
E	Leon Edel's Collection, Honolulu, Hawaii
FH	Books whose whereabouts are unknown but whose titles have been derived from the three Fabes catalogues and the Hodgson list
H	The Houghton Library, Harvard University, Cambridge, Massachusetts
HL	Harry Levin's Collection, Cambridge, Massachusetts
L	Henry James's Collection, Lamb House, Rye, Sussex, England
ML	Mark Samuels Lasner's Collection, Washington, D.C.
P	Princeton University Library, Princeton, New Jersey
T	Adeline R. Tintner's Collection, New York, New York
W	Stanley Wertheim's Collection, New York, New York

Figure 1. Lamb House, Upstairs Winter Writing Room
This room contains rare bindings, with framed originals of illustrations for
"An International Episode." Describing this room in a letter to Mrs. W. G.
Smalley, James wrote:

> I am writing in a little sunny upstairs winter writing room which, oh
> how I wish, I could usher and ensconce you. It has an old old
> panelling to within a couple of feet of old flower'd or butterflied
> paper. The panelling is all painted green (awfully soothing I find)
> and there are nice old fashioned cupboards and an old Dutch-tiled
> fireplace. One window looks into the garden, and the other into a
> big clean Dutch looking court and over it and beyond it to Win-
> chelsea and Hastings.

(Collection Leon Edel)

A

About, Edmond. *Madelon*. Paris, 1885.   0-FH

Adams, Brooks. *The Emancipation of Massachusetts*. Boston:
Houghton, Mifflin, 1887.   A-H

————. *The Law of Civilization and Decay*. London: Swan
Sonnenschein; New York: Macmillan, 1895.   0-H

Adams, Charles Francis. *Trans-Atlantic Historical Solidarity*.
Oxford: Clarendon, 1913.   0-H

Adams, Henry. *Democracy*. New York: Henry Holt, 1880.   A-P

Addison, Joseph. *Essays of Joseph Addison*. 1880.   A-FH

Ainger, Alfred. *Crabbe*. London: Macmillan and Company,
1903.   A-BAR

Albemarle, Earl of. *Fifty Years of My Life*. 1876.   0-FH

Alexis, Paul. *Emile Zola*. Paris: Charpentier, 1882.   0-T

Allen, T. *History of Surrey and Sussex*. 1829.   A-FH

Amiel, Henri Frédéric. *Fragments d'un journal intime*.
Paris, 1884.   A-FH

Ampère, J. *L'Histoire romaine à Rome*. Paris: M. Lévy,
1863–64.   0-FH

Apuleius. *The Golden Ass*. Trans. William Adlington (1568).
Tudor Translations, 1893.   0-FH

Arabian Nights' Entertainments. Trans. E. W. Lane. 1839–41.   A-FH

Arnold, Matthew. *Discourses in America*. 1885.   A-FH

————. *Edmund Burke on Irish Affairs*. 1881.   A-FH

————. *Essays in Criticism*. Boston: Ticknor and Fields,
1865.   A-L

————. *Essays in Criticism*. London: Macmillan, 1869.   A-H

————. *Friendship's Garland*. London: Smith, Elder
& Co., 1871.   A-H

————. *God and the Bible: A Review of Objections to
'Literature and Dogma.'* New York: Macmillan, 1875.   A-L

————. *Irish Essays*. 1882.   A-FH

————. *Last Essays on Church and Religion*. New York:
Macmillan, 1877.   A-L

————. *Letters*. 1885.   A-FH

————. *Literature and Dogma*. 1873.   A-FH

————. *Mixed Essays*. 1879.   A-FH

————. *On the Study of Celtic Literature*. London: Smith,
Elder & Co., 1867.   0-L

————. *Poetical Works*. 1890.   A-FH

Augier, Emile. *L'Aventurière*. Paris: Calmann-Lévy, n.d.   A-BAR
————. *Oeuvres diverses*. Paris: C. Lévy, 1876–83.   0-FH
————. *Théâtre complet*. Paris: C. Lévy, 1876–83.   0-FH
Austen, Jane. *Letters of Jane Austen*. London: Richard
    Bentley, 1884.   A-H
Austen-Leigh, J. E. *Memoir of Jane Austen*. 1906.   0-FH

B

Bagehot, Walter. *Biographical Studies*. London: Longmans,
    Green, 1889.   A-H
————. *Economic Studies*. London: Longmans, Green, 1888.   A-H
————. *Literary Studies*. London: Longmans, Green, 1888.   A-H
Balestier, Wolcott [See also Kipling, *The Naulahka*]. *The
    Average Woman*. With A Biographical Sketch by Henry
    James. London: William Heinemann, 1892.   A-BAR
Balfour, Arthur James. *The Foundations of Belief*. London:
    Longmans, Green and Co., 1895.   A-L
Balzac, Honoré de. *Les Contes drolatiques*. Paris: Garnier
    Frères, n.d.   A-E
————. *Correspondance*. Paris: Calmann Lévy, 1876.   A-E
————. *Oeuvres complètes*. Paris: Calmann Lévy, 1896.   0-BAR
————. *Thèâtre complet*. Paris: Michel Lévy Frères,
    1869–1874.   0-BAR
Barbey d'Aurevilly, Jules-Amédée. *Du dandysme*. Paris:
    A. Lemerre, 1879.   0-FH
Bardoux, A. *La Comtesse Pauline de Beaumont*. Paris:
    Calmann Lévy, 1884.   A-BAR
————. *Madame de Custine*. Paris, 1891.   0-FH
Bargagli, Scipione. *Le Novelle*. Siena: Ignazio Gati, 1873.   A-BAR
Barine, Arvède. *Névrosés*. 1898.   0-FH
————. *Portraits de femmes*. Paris, 1887.   0-FH
————. *Princesses et grandes dames*. 1890.   0-FH
Barrès, Maurice. *L'Ame Française et la Guerre; L'Union
    Sacrée*. Paris: Emile-Paul Frères, 1915.   0-BL
————. *Du Sang, de la volupté et de la mort*. Paris:
    Charpentier, 1894.   A-T
Barrie, Sir James Matthew. *Margaret Ogilvy*. London: Hodder
    and Stoughton, 1897.   A-H
————. *Tommy and Grizel*. London: Cassell, 1900.   A-H
Barrière, Marcel. *L'Oeuvre de Honoré de Balzac*. Paris:
    Calmann Lévy, 1890.   A-T

Bashkirtseff, Marie. *Journal.* Paris: G. Charpentier, 1890.   A-FH
Baudelaire, Charles. *Les Fleurs du mal.* Paris: M. Lévy, 1872.   A-FH
Becque, Henri. *Théâtre complet.* Paris: Charpentier, 1890.   0-FH
Beerbohm, Max. *A Christmas Garland.* 1911.   0-FH
Bell, Currer. *Villette.* 1854.   A-FH
Benedict, Clare. *A Resemblance and Other Stories.* New York:
Putnam's, 1909.   0-FH
Benson, Arthur Christopher. *Babylonica.* Eton: George
New, 1895.   A-H
———. *Essays.* London: William Heinemann, 1896.   0-L
Bergerat, Emile. *L'Amour en république.* Paris: E. Dentu,
1889.   0-FH
———. *Figarismes de Caliban.* Paris, 1888.   0-FH
———. *Grands Ecrivains français, Froissart, Madame de
Staël.* 1890–98.   0-FH
———. *Le Livre de Caliban.* Paris, 1887.   0-FH
———. *La Lyre comique.* Paris, 1889.   0-FH
———. *Le Rire de Caliban.* Paris, n.d..   0-FH
———. *Théophile Gautier.* Paris, 1879.   0-FH
Bernard, Charles de. *Gerfaut.* Paris: M. Lévy, 1864.   A-BAR
Bernstein, Henry. *La Rafale.* Paris: Librairie Charpentier et
Fasquelle, 1906.   A-BAR
Besant, Sir Walter. *Early London.* London: Adam and Charles
Black, 1908.   A-BAR
———. *East London.* London: Chatto & Windus, 1903.   A-BAR
———. *London.* London: Chatto & Windus, 1904.   A-BAR
———. *London City.* London: Adam & Charles Black, 1910.   A-BAR
———. *London in the Eighteenth Century.* London: Adam &
Charles Black, 1903.   A-BAR
———. *London in the Nineteenth Century.* London: Adam &
Charles Black, 1908.   A-BAR
———. *London in the Time of the Stuarts.* London: Adam &
Charles Black, 1903.   A-BAR
———. *London in the Time of the Tudors.* London: Adam &
Charles Black, 1904.   A-BAR
———. *London North of the Thames.* London: Adam &
Charles Black, 1904.   A-BAR
———. *London South of the Thames.* London: Adam &
Charles Black, 1904.   A-BAR
———. *Mediaeval London.* London: Adam & Charles
Black, 1906.   A-BAR
———. *South London.* London: Chatto & Windus, 1901.   A-BAR

————. *Westminster*. London: Chatto & Windus, 1895.   A-BAR
Betham-Edwards, Matilda. *The Lord of the Harvest*. London:
Hurst & Blackett, 1899.   0-T
Beugnot, Comte du. *Mémoires (1783–1815)*. Paris:
E. Dentu, 1868.   A-BAR
Bible. O. T. Isaiah i-xxxix. English. Authorized. London:
Macmillan, 1883.   A-H
Bigarré, Gal. *Mémoires du Gal. Bigarré, aide de camp du Roi
Joseph 1775–1813*. Paris: Ernest Kolb, n.d.   A-BAR
Binns, H. B. *Life of Walt Whitman*. 1905.   A-FH
Birrell, Augustine. *Collected Essays*. London: Elliot Stock,
1899.   A-L
————. *Essays about Men, Women, etc.* 1894.   0-FH
————. *Obiter Dicta*. 1884.   0-FH
————. *Sir Frank Lockwood*. 1898.   0-FH
Blomfield, Reginald. *History of Renaissance Architecture in
England*. 1897.   0-FH
Boccaccio, Giovanni. *Il Decameron*. Florence, 1825.   A-FH
Bodley, John Edward Courtenay. *France*. London: Macmillan
and Company, 1898.   A-BAR
Bordeaux, Henry. *Les Ecrivains et les moeurs*. Paris, 1900.   0-FH
Borrow, George. *Celebrated Trials . . . from the Earliest
Records to 1825*. 1825.   0-FH
Boswell, James. *The Life of Samuel Johnson*. London: John
Murray, 1883.   A-H
————. *The Life of Samuel Johnson, LL. D.* London: Baldwin
& Son, 1799.   A-T
Bourget, Paul. *André Cornélis*. Paris: Lemerre, 1887.   0-T
————. *Un Coeur de femme*. Paris: Lemerre, 1890.   0-T
————. *Cosmopolis*. Paris: Lemerre, 1893.   0-T
————. *Un Crime d'amour*. Paris: Lemerre, 1886.   0-T
————. *Cruelle Enigme*. Paris: 1885.   0-T
————. *La Dame qui a perdu son peintre*. Paris: 1910.   0-FH
————. *Les Détours du coeur*. Paris: n.d.   0-FH
————. *Le Disciple*. Paris: Lemerre, 1889.   0-T
————. *Un Divorce*. Paris: Plon, 1904.   A-T
————. *Un Divorce*. Paris: n.d.   0-FH
————. *Drames de famille*. Paris: Librairie Plon, 1900.   0-T
————. *Edel*. Paris: Lemerre, 1878.   0-T
————. *L'Emigré*. Paris: Librairie Plon, 1907.   A-H
————. *L'Envers du Décor*. Paris: Plon, 1911.   A-T
————. *Essais de psychologie contemporaine*. Paris:
Lemerre, 1883.   A-T

_____. *L'Etape*. Paris: Plon-Nourrit et Cie, 1902.   A-BAR
_____. *Etudes et portraits*. Paris: Lemerre, 1889.   0-T
_____. *Le Fantôme*. Paris: Librairie Plon, n.d.   A-T
_____. *Un Homme d'affaires*. Paris: Librairie Plon, 1900.   0-T
_____. *Une Idylle tragique*. Paris: Lemerre, 1896.   0-T
_____. *L'Irréparable*. Paris: Lemerre, 1884.   0-T
_____. *Mensonges*. Paris: Lemerre, 1890.   0-T
_____. *Nouveaux Pastels*. Paris: Lemerre, 1891.   0-T
_____. *Outre-mer*. Paris: Lemerre, 1895.   0-T
_____. *Pastels*. Paris: Lemerre, 1889.   A-T
_____. *Poésies*. 1885–87.   0-FH
_____. *Psychologie contemporaine*. Paris: Lemerre, 1886.   0-T
_____. *Un Scrupule*. Paris: Lemerre, 1893.   0-T
_____. *Le Sens de la mort*. Paris: Plon, 1915.   A-T
_____. *Sensations d'Italie*. 1891.   A-T
_____. *La Terre promise*. Paris: Lemerre, 1892.   0-T
_____. *Le Tribun*. Paris: Librairie Plon, 1912.   A-T
Brandes, G. *William Shakespeare*. 1898.   A-FH
Brantôme, Pierre de Bourdeilles, Seigneur de. *Oeuvres*. Paris:
   Aux Depens du Libraire, 1779.   A-T
Bridges, Robert. *The Spirit of Man: An Anthology*. 1916.   0-FH
Brieux, Eugène. *Blanchette: Comédie en Trois Actes*. Paris:
   Calmann-Lévy, 1907.   A-BL
_____. *Les Avariés: Pièce en Trois Actes*. Paris: P.-V.
   Stock, 1907.   A-BL
Brontë, Charlotte. *The Professor*. London: Smith, Elder, 1857.   A-T
Brontë Sisters. *Works: Jane Eyre and Shirley*. 1899.   0-FH
Brooke, Margaret (The Ranee of Sarawak). *My Life in
   Sarawak*. 1913.   0-FH
Brooke, S. A. *History of Early English Literature*. London:
   Macmillan, 1892.   A-FH
Brown, Horatio F. *In and Around Venice*. London:
   Rivingtons, 1905.   A-T
_____. *John Addington Symonds. A Biography*. London: John
   C. Nimmo, 1895.   A-BAR
_____. *Life on the Lagoons*. 1884.   0-FH
Browning, Robert [See also Orr]. *Asolando*. 1890.   A-FH
_____. *Dramatic Idyls*. 1879.   A-FH
_____. *Dramatis Personae*. Boston, 1864.   A-FH
_____. *Ferishtah's Fancies*. 1884.   A-FH
_____. *The Inn Album*. 1875.   A-FH
_____. *Letters of Robert Browning and Elizabeth Barrett*.
   1899.   A-FH

_____. *Men and Women.* 1855.   0-FH

_____. *Poetical Works.* 1884–94.   0-FH

_____. *The Ring and the Book.* 1868–69.   0-FH

_____. *Sordello, Strafford, Christmas-Eve and Easter-Day.*
Boston: Ticknor and Fields, 1864.   A-BAR

Brunetière, Ferdinand. *Etudes critiques sur l'histoire de la
littérature française.* Paris: Hachette, 1899.   A-T

_____. *Histoire et littérature, vol. 3.* Paris: Calmann Lévy,
1898.   A-T

Bryce, James. *The American Commonwealth.* London:
Macmillan, 1888.   A-H

_____. *Transcaucasia and Ararat.* 1879.   A-FH

Bullen, A. H. *Lyrics from Elizabethan Song-Books.* 1887.   0-FH

Bulwer, Edward Lord Lytton. *Conversations with an Ambitious
Student in Ill Health.* New York, 1832.   A-FH

_____. *The Life, Letters and Library Remains of Edward
Bulwer, Lord Lytton.* London: Kegan Paul, Trench and
Company, 1883.   A-BAR

_____. *My Novel.* Edinburgh and London: William
Blackwood and Sons, 1853.   A-BAR

Bunyan, John. *Pilgrim's Progress.* London: Longman, Green,
Longman, and Roberts, 1860.   A-H

Burckhardt, J. *The Renaissance in Italy.* 1878.   A-FH

Burke, J. B. *Romantic Records of Distinguished Families.*
1851.   0-FH

Burne-Jones, Edward. *Memorials of, by G. B-J.* New York:
The Macmillan Company, 1904.   A-BAR

Burney, Fanny (Mme. D'Arblay). *Diary and Letters of
Madame D'Arblay.* London: Henry Colburn, 1842–46.   A-BAN

Burton, R. F. *Pilgrimage to El-Medinah.* 1855.   A-FH

Busch, Dr. M. *Bismarck: Some Secret Pages of His History.*
1898.   A-FH

Busnach, William. *Trois pièces.* Paris, 1884.   0-FH

Butler, Frances Anne Kemble [See also Kemble]. *Journal.*
London: John Murray, 1835.   A-BAR

Butler, Sir W. F. *Sir William Butler, an Autobiography.*
London: Constable and Company, Ltd., 1911.   A-BAR

Byron, Lord. *The Works of Lord Byron, with His Letters and
Journals, and His Life by Thomas Moore.* London: Murray,
1886.   0-FH

C

Cabot, James Elliot. *A Memoir of Ralph Waldo Emerson.*
London: Macmillan, 1887.   A-BAR

Camp, Maxime du. *Souvenirs littéraires.* Paris: Librairie
Hachette et Cie, 1882–83.   A-BAR

Campbell, J. D. *Samuel Taylor Coleridge.* 1894.   0-FH

Carlyle, Jane Welsh. *Early Letters of Jane Welsh Carlyle.*
London, 1889.   A-FH

———. *Letters and Memorials.* 1883.   A-FH

———. *New Letters.* 1903.   A-FH

Carlyle, Thomas. *Correspondence between Goethe and Carlyle.*
1887.   A-FH

———. *Early Letters of Thomas Carlyle.* Ed. Charles Eliot
Norton. London: Macmillan, 1886.   A-BAN

———. *The French Revolution.* London: James Fraser, 1839.   A-H

———. *History of Frederick the Great.* 1870–71.   A-FH

———. *Letters of Thomas Carlyle, 1826–32.* London:
Macmillan, 1888.   A-BAN

———. *Reminiscences.* Ed. J. A. Froude. 1881.   A-FH

———. *Reminiscences of My Irish Journey in 1849.* 1882.   A-FH

———. *Wilhelm Meister's Apprenticeship and Travels.*
Boston, 1865.   A-FH

Carlyle, Thomas and Ralph Waldo Emerson. *Correspondence
(1834–72).* Boston: Osgood, 1883.   A-BAR

———. *Oliver Cromwell's Letters and Speeches.* 1870.   A-FH

Casanova, Jacques. *Mémoires.* Paris: Garnier, n.d.   A-T

Cellini, Benvenuto. *Cellini.* Trans. J. A. Symonds. London, 1888.   A-H

Cerfberr et Christophe. *Répertoire de la Comédie humaine de
Honoré de Balzac.* Paris: Calmann Lévy, 1887.   A-T

Cervantes, Miguel de. *Don Quixote.* 1866.   0-FH

Champneys, Basil. *A Quiet Corner of England.* London: Seeley,
Jackson, and Halliday, 1875.   A-H

Chaptal, Comte. *Mes souvenirs sur Napoléon.* Paris: Librairie
Plon, E. Plon, Nourrit et Cie, 1893.   A-BAR

Chaucer, Geoffrey. *The Poetical Works of Geoffrey Chaucer.*
London: Bell and Daldy, 1866.   A-H

Chesterfield, Lord. *Letters Written by the Late Right Honourable
Philip Dormer.* London: J. Dodsley, 1793.   A-L

Chesterton, G. K. *Charles Dickens.* 1906.   A-FH

_____. *George Bernard Shaw.* 1910.   0-FH

_____. *Heretics.* 1906.   A-FH

_____. *Twelve Types.* A. L. Humphreys, 1902.   0-FH

Chevrillon, André. *Dans l'Inde.* Paris: Librairie Hachette et
  Cie, 1891.   A-BAR

Childs, George W. *Recollections.* Philadelphia: Lippincott, 1891.   A-T

Church, R. W. *Bacon.* London: Macmillan, 1888.   A-T

Churchill, Charles. *Works.* 1774.   0-FH

Churchill, Sir Winston Spencer. *Lord Randolph Churchill.*
  London: Macmillan, 1906.   A-H

Cibber, Colley. *Apology for his Life.* J. C. Nimmo, 1889.   A-FH

Clément, Charles. *Michel-Ange, Leonard de Vinci, Raphael.*
  Paris: Hetzel, 1867.   A-BL

Clifford, Ethel. *Songs of Dream.* 1903.   0-FH

_____. *A Wild Proxy.* 1893.   0-FH

Clifford, Mrs. W. K. *Aunt Anne.* London: Richard Bentley and
  Son, 1891.   A-BAR

_____. *A Flash of Summer.* 1895.   0-FH

_____. *The Last Touches.* 1892.   0-FH

_____. *Love-Letters of a Worldly Woman.* London: Edward
  Arnold, 1891.   A-BAR

_____. *The Modern Way.* London: Chapman and Hall, 1906.   A-H

_____. *Sir George's Objections.* 1910.   0-FH

_____. *A Woman Alone.* London: Methuen, 1901.   A-H

_____. *Woodside Farm.* 1902.   A-H

Clifton et Grimaux. *Dictionnaire Anglais-Français.* Paris:
  Garnier, n.d.   0-FH

Clive, Caroline (Wigley). *Paul Ferroll.* London: Saunders and
  Otley, 1856.   A-H

Clough, A. H. *Greek History from Themistocles to Alexander.*
  London: Longman, Green, Longman, and Roberts, 1860.   A-BAR

Cobbett, William. *Rural Rides in the Counties of Surrey,
  Kent . . . 1853.* London: A. Cobbett, 1853.   A-H

Coleridge, Samuel Taylor. *Poetical Works.* 1893.   0-FH

Collins, J. C. *Bolingbroke.* 1886.   A-FH

_____. *Essays and Studies.* 1895.   A-FH

_____. *Jonathan Swift.* 1893.   0-FH

Congreve, William. *Works.* Birmingham: J. Baskerville, 1761.   A-FH

Conrad, Joseph. *The Nigger of the "Narcissus."* London: William
  Heinemann, 1898.   A-H

_____. *Under Western Eyes.* London: Methuen, 1911.   0-H

Constant, Benjamin. *Adolphe.* A. Quantin, 1878.   A-FH
_____. *Journal intime.* P. Ollendorf, 1895.   A-FH
_____. *Lettres à Mme Récamier.* 1882.   A-FH
Cook, E. T. *Life of John Ruskin.* 1911.   A-FH
Cooper, J. F. *The Monikins: A Tale.* London: Richard
  Bentley, 1835.   0-L
Cooper, W. D. *History of Winchelsea.* 1850.   A-FH
Coppée, François. *Henriette.* Paris: Alphonse Lemerre, 1889.   A-BAR
_____. *L'Homme, la vie.* 1889.   A-FH
_____. *Longues et brèves.* Paris: Alphonse Lemerre, 1893.   A-BAR
_____. *Les Vrais riches.* Paris: Alphonse Lemerre, n.d.   A-BAR
Cornwall, Barry (pseud. of Procter, Bryan Waller). *English
  Songs.* London: G. Bell and Sons, 1880.   A-BAR
Corréard et Savigny. *Naufrage de la frégate La Méduse.* 1821.   A-T
Cousin, Victor. *Madame de Chevreuse et Madame de Hautefort.*
  Paris: Didier, 1856.   A-FH
_____. *Madame de Longueville.* Paris: Didier, 1853.   A-FH
Cowper, The Honorable Spencer, ed. *Diary of Mary Countess
  Cowper.* London: John Murray, 1865.   A-BAR
Cowper, William. *Works, with Life by R. Southey.* 1836–37.   0-FH
Crabbe, George. *Life and Poems of the Rev. George Crabbe.*
  London: Murray, 1836.   A-T
Craik, H. *Life of Jonathan Swift.* 1882.   0-FH
Crane, Stephen. *The Red Badge of Courage.* London:
  Heinemann, 1896.   A-W
Crawford, Francis Marion. *Gleanings from Venetian History.*
  1905.   A-FH
_____. *Saracinesca.* 1897.   0-FH
Créqui, Renée-Caroline de Froullay, Marquise de. *Souvenirs de
  la Marquise de Créqui de 1710 à 1803.* Paris: H. L. Delloye,
  1840.   A-BAR
Cross, John Walter. *George Eliot's Life as Related in Her Letters
  and Journals.* 1885.   A-FH
Croze, Pierre de. *Le Chevalier de Boufflers, etc.* Paris, 1894.   A-FH
Cunningham, Sir H. S. *Lord Bowen: A Biographical Sketch.*
  1896.   0-FH

D

D'Annunzio, Gabriel. *L'Innocente.* Naples: Ferdinando
  Bideri, 1892.   A-BAR

_____. *Il Piacere*. Milan: Fratelli Treves, 1898.   A-BAR

_____. *Trionfo della morte*. Milan: Fratelli Treves, 1894.   0-BAR

_____. *Le Vergini delle Rocce*. Milan: Fratelli Treves, 1898.   A-BAR

Dante. *La Divina Commedia*. Florence, 1874.   A-FH

_____. *The Divine Comedy: Purgatory and Paradise*. Boston,
1891–92.   0-FH

_____. *The Inferno*. 1865.   0-FH

Darmesteter, Mary J. *La Vie de Ernest Renan*. Paris: C.
Lévy, 1898.   A-BAR

Darwin, Frances. *The Life and Letters of Charles Darwin*.
London: John Murray, 1887.   A-BAR

Daudet, Alphonse. *Contes du lundi*. Paris, 1882.   0-FH

_____. *Entre les frises et la rampe*. Paris, 1894.   0-FH

_____. *L'Evangéliste*. Paris, 1883.   0-FH

_____. *Froment jeune et Risler ainé*. Paris: Charpentier, 1881.   A-T

_____. *L'Immortel: moeurs parisiennes*. Paris: Alphonse
Lemerre, 1888.   A-L

_____. *Jack*. Paris: Charpentier, 1882.   A-T

_____. *La Menteuse: Pièce tirée de la nouvelle publiée*. Paris:
Ernest Flammarion, n.d.   A-L

_____. *Le Nabab*. Paris: Charpentier, 1886.   A-T

_____. *Numa Roumestan*. Paris: Charpentier, 1887.   A-T

_____. *Oeuvres complètes*. Paris: Charpentier, 1891–97.   A-FH

_____. *La Petite Paroisse*. Paris: Lemerre, 1895.   A-T

_____. *Les Rois en exil*. Paris: Charpentier, 1885.   A-T

_____. *Rose et Ninette: Moeurs du jour*. Paris: Librairie E.
Flammarion, n.d.   A-L

_____. *Sapho*. Paris: Charpentier, 1884.   A-T

_____. *Souvenirs d'un homme de lettres*. Paris: C. Marpon et
E. Flammarion, n.d.   A-L

_____. *Tartarin de Tarascon; Lettres de mon moulin*. Paris:
Charpentier, 1884.   A-T

_____. *Tartarin sur les Alpes*. Paris, 1888.   0-FH

_____. *Trente ans de Paris: à travers ma vie et mes livres*.
Paris: C. Marpon, 1888.   A-L

_____. *Le Trésor d'Arlatan*. Paris: Librairie Charpentier et
Fasquelle, 1897.   A-H

Daudet, Léon. *Alphonse Daudet*. Paris: Bibliothèque-Charpentier,
1898.   A-BAR

_____. *Les Idées en marche*. 1896.   0-FH

_____. *Les "Kamtchatka."* Paris: Bibliothèque-Charpentier,
1895.   A-BAR

_____. *La Lutte*. Paris: Bibliothèque-Charpentier, 1907.   A-H

_____. *La Mésentente*. Paris: Bibliothèque-Charpentier, 1911.   A-BAR
_____. *La Romance du temps present*. Paris: Charpentier, 1900.   0-T
_____. *Le Partage de l'enfant*. Paris: Charpentier, 1905.   0-T
_____. *Le Voyage de Shakespeare*. Paris, 1896.   0-FH
Daudet, Madame Alphonse. *Au bord des Terrasses. Poésies.*
Paris: Lemerre, 1906.   0-T
Daudet, Lucien Alphonse. *Le Chemin mort*. Paris: Ernest
Flammarion, n.d.   A-BAR
_____. *la Fourmilière*. Paris: Ernest Flammarion, n.d.   A-BAR
_____. *Journées de femme*. Paris: Bibliothèque-Charpentier,
1898.   A-BAR
D'Aulnoy, Marie-Catherine, Comtesse. *La Cour et la ville de
Madrid*. Paris: E. Plon et Cie, 1874–76.   A-BAR
Davies, John Llewelyn. *Theology and Morality*. London:
King, 1873.   A-H
De Brosses, C. *Lettres familières (1739–40)*. Paris: Librairie
Académique, 1869.   A-BAR
Defoe, Daniel. *The Novels and Miscellaneous Works*. Oxford:
Printed by D. A. Talboys, for Thomas Tegg, 1840.   A-BAR
De Genlis, Madame. *Mémoires*. Ladrocat, 1825.   0-FH
De Heredia, J. M. *Les Trophées*. Paris: A. Lemerre, 1893.   0-FH
De Quincey, Thomas. *The Collected Writings of Thomas de
Quincey*. Introd. David Masson. Edinburgh: Adam and Charles
Black, 1889–90.   A-L
De Senancourt, Etienne Pivert. *Obermann*. Paris: Charpentier,
1865.   A-FH
De Vogüé, Vicomte E. Melchior. *Le Maître de la mer*. Paris:
Librairie Plon, 1903.   A-BAR
_____. *Les Morts qui parlent*. 1899.   0-FH
_____. *Le Rappel des ombres*. Paris: 1900.   0-FH
_____. *Remarques du centenaire*. Paris: 1889.   A-FH
_____. *Le Roman Russe*. Paris: E. Plon, 1886.   A-T
Delacroix, Eugène. *Journal*. Paris: E. Plon, 1893.   A-BAR
_____. *Lettres*. Paris: 1878.   A-FH
Delzant, Alidor. *Paul de Saint-Victor*. Paris: 1886.   0-FH
Dennistoun, J. *The Dukes of Urbino*. 1851.   A-FH
D'Epinay. *Mémoires de Madame d'Epinay*. Paris: G. Charpentier,
ca. 1885.   A-H
Desnoirresterres, Gustave. *Voltaire et la société au XVIIIᵉ siècle*.
Paris: Librairie Académique, 1871–76.   A-BAR
D'Haussonville, Le Comte. *Ma jeunesse: souvenirs*. 1882.   A-FH
D'Heylli, G. *Rachel d'après sa correspondance*. 1882.   A-FH

D'Humières, Robert. *Lettres Volées*. Paris: Librairie Félix
Juven, n.d.   A-T

Dickens, Charles. *The Chimes*. London: Chapman and
Hall, 1845.   A-H

_____. *Dombey and Son*. London: Macmillan, 1900.   A-BAN

_____. *Life and Adventures of Nicholas Nickleby*. London:
Macmillan, 1900.   A-BAN

Dickinson, G. Lowes. *A Modern Symposium*. 1906.   A-T.

_____. *Religion and Immortality*. Boston, 1911.   A-FH

Diderot, Denis. *Le Neveu de Rameau*. Paris: A. Quantin, 1883. 0-FH

_____. *Oeuvres choisies*. Paris: Librairie des Bibliophiles,
1877–79.   A-FH

Digby, Sir Kenelm. *Castrations from the Private Memoirs of Sir
Kenelm Digby*. London: 1828.   0-H

_____. *Private Memoirs of Sir Kenelm Digby*. London:
Saunders and Otley, 1827.   A-H

Dixon, W. H. *Her Majesty's Tower*. 1885.   0-FH

Dobson, Austin. *At Prior Park*. 1912.   A-FH

_____. *At the Sign of the Lyre*. 1886.   0-FH

_____. *Eighteenth Century Vignettes*. First Series. 1892.   A-FH

_____. *Eighteenth Century Vignettes*. Third Series. London:
Chatto & Windus, 1896.   A-L

_____. *Eighteenth Century Vignettes*. London: Chatto &
Windus, 1902.   A-L

_____. *Fielding*. 1883.   A-FH

_____. *Horace Walpole: a Memoir*. London, 1893.   A-FH

_____. *Old World Idylls*. London, 1893.   A-FH

_____. *Side-Walk Studies*. London: Chatto & Windus, 1902.   A-L

_____. *William Hogarth*. 1891.   0-FH

Donnay, Maurice. *La Douloureuse*. 1897.   0-FH

Doran, Dr. *Monarchs Retired From Business*. London: Richard
Bentley, 1857.   0-T

_____. *Saints and Sinners*. 1868.   A-FH

Dostoevski, Fedor Mikhailovich. *Souvenirs de la maison des
morts*. Paris: Librairie Plon, E. Plon, Nourrit, 1886.   A-H

Doudan, Xavier. *Mélanges et lettres*. Paris: Calmann Lévy, 1876. A-BAR

Dowden, E. *Life of Percy Bysshe Shelley*. n.d.   0-FH

Doyle, Arthur Conan. *The Valley of Fear*. 1915.   0-FH

Droz, Antoine-Gustave. *Babolain*. 1872.   0-FH

Dumas, Alexandre. *La Femme de Claude*. Paris: Michel Lévy
Frères, 1873.   0-BAR

_____. *Les Trois Mousquetaires*. Paris: Calmann Lévy, 1892. A-T

_____. *Les Trois Mousquetaires.* Vol. II. Paris: Calmann-Lévy,
1899.   0-BL

_____. *Vingt ans après.* Paris: Calmann Lévy, 1893.   A-T

Dumas, Alexandre (Fils). *Monsieur Alphonse.* Paris: Michel
Lévy Frères, 1874.   0-BAR

_____. *La Princesse Georges.* Paris, 1872.   A-FH

_____. *Théâtre complet.* Paris: Calmann Lévy, 1886.   A-T

Du Maurier, George. *Peter Ibbetson.* 1891.   A-H

_____. *Trilby.* London: Osgood, McIlvaine, 1894.   A-H

Duruy, J. *Mémoires de Barrès.* Paris: Hachette, 1895–96.   0-FH

E

Eliot, George. *Adam Bede.*   A-FH

_____. *Daniel Deronda.*   A-FH

_____. *Essays.*   A-FH

_____. *Jubal.*   A-FH

_____. *Middlemarch.*   A-FH

_____. *The Mill on the Floss.*   A-FH

_____. *Silas Marner.*   A-FH

_____. *The Spanish Gypsy.* Edinburgh and London: William
Blackwood & Sons, 1868.   A-BAR

_____. *Theophrastus Such.*   A-FH

Elton, Oliver. *Michael Drayton.* 1905.   A-FH

Emerson, Ralph Waldo [See also Carlyle]. *Emerson Centenary in
Concord/May 25, 1903.* Concord, 1903.   0-FH

_____. *Essays.* London: Macmillan, 1885.   A-H

_____. *Journals, 1820–32.* London: Constable, 1909.   A-FH

_____. *Journals of Ralph Waldo Emerson.* Boston: Houghton
Mifflin, 1910.   A-H

_____. *Journals of Ralph Waldo Emerson.* London: Constable,
1909.   A-H

_____. *Natural History of Intellect.* Boston: Houghton
Mifflin, 1904.   A-H

Erckmann-Chatrian [Emile Erckmann and Alexandre Chatrian].
L'Ami Fritz. 1865.   A-FH

_____. *Contes de la montagne.* 1860.   A-FH

_____. *Les Deux frères.* 1860–73.   A-FH

Evelyn, John. *Diary.* 1879.

Eyre, Lieut. V. *Military Operations at Cabul.* 1843.   0-FH

F

Fawcett, Edgar. *A Romance of Old New York*. Philadelphia: Lippincott, 1897.	0-T
Ferrier, Susan. *Marriage*. Bentley, 1841.	A-FH
Ferry, G. *Balzac et ses amis*. 1888.	0-FH
Feuillet, Octave. *Le Journal d'une femme*. Paris: C. Lévy, 1878.	A-FH
_____. *Quelques années de ma vie*. 1894.	0-FH
_____. *Le Sphinx*. Paris: Michel Lévy Frères, 1874.	0-BAR
Fielding, Henry. *Amelia*. London: James Cochrane, 1832.	A-E
_____. *Joseph Andrews*. London: James Cochrane, 1832.	A-BAR
_____. *The Soul of a People*. 1899.	A-FH
Filon, Augustine. *Mérimée et ses amis*. Paris: Hachette, 1894.	0-FH
_____. *Profils anglais: Randolph Churchill, Joseph Chamberlain*. Paris, 1893.	A-BAR
Findlater, J. H. *Stones from a Glass House*. 1904.	A-FH
Fiske, John. *American Political Ideas*. London: Macmillan, 1885.	A-H
_____. *The Idea of God as Affected by Modern Knowledge*. Boston: Houghton Mifflin, 1890.	A-H
Fitzgerald, C. *Venetia Victrix (Poems)*. 1889.	0-FH
Fitzgerald, Edward. *Letters*. London: Macmillan, 1894.	A-BAR
_____. *Letters to Fanny Kemble*. E. Bentley, 1895.	A-T
_____. *More Letters of. . . .* London: Macmillan, 1901.	0-BAR
_____. *The Rubaiyat of Omar Khayam*. 1900.	0-FH
Fitzgerald, P. *Life of John Wilkes*. 1888.	A-FH
Fitzmaurice, Edmond George Petty-Fitzmaurice. *The Life of Granville George Leveson Gower*. London: Longmans, Green, 1905.	A-H
Flaubert, Gustave. *Bouvard et Pécuchet: Oeuvre posthume*. Paris: Alphonse Lemerre, 1881.	A-L
_____. *Le Candidat*. Paris: Charpentier, 1874.	A-FH
_____. *Oeuvres complètes*. A. Quantin, 1885.	A-FH
_____. *Trois contes*. Paris: G. Charpentier, 1877.	A-L
Fleming, George (Constance Fletcher). *Little Stories about Women*. London: Grant Richards, 1897.	A-T
Fletcher, Horace. *The New Glutton or Epicure*. London: B. F. Stevens and Brown; New York: Frederick A. Stokes, ca. 1899, 1903.	A-BAR
Forbes, A. *My Experiences of the War between France and Germany*. 1871.	A-FH
Ford, John. *Dramatic Works*. 1827.	0-FH
Forneron, Henri. *Les Ducs de Guise*. Paris: E. Plon, 1893.	A-FH

_____. *Louise de Kerouaille, duchesse de Portsmouth.* Paris:
Librairie Plon, 1886.   A-T
France, Anatole. *Balthasar.* Paris, 1889.   A-FH
_____. *Clio.* Paris: Calmann Lévy, 1900.   A-L
_____. *Les Désirs de Jean Servein.* 1882.   0-FH
_____. *Les Dieux ont soif.* Paris, 1912.   A-FH
_____. *L'Ile des pingouins.* 1907.   -0-FH
_____. *Le Livre de mon ami.* 1885.   0-FH
_____. *Le Lys rouge.* 1894.   0-FH
_____. *Le Puits de Sainte Claire.* Paris, 1893.   A-FH
_____. *La Révolte des anges.* 1914.   0-FH
_____. *La Rôtisserie de la Reine Pédauque.* Paris, 1893.   A-FH
_____. *La Vie de Jeanne d'Arc.* Paris: Calmann-Lévy, n.d.   A-T
Freeman, E. A. *Historical and Architectural Sketches.* 1876.   A-FH
_____. *Subject and Neighbor Lands of Venice.* 1881.   A-FH
_____. *William the Conqueror.* London: Macmillan, 1888.   A-H
Fromentin, Eugène. *Dominique.* 1863.   A-FH
_____. *Les Maîtres d'autrefois.* Paris: E. Plon, 1876.   A-H
Froude, James Anthony. *The Council of Trent.* 1896.   A-FH
_____. *English Seamen in the Sixteenth Century.* London:
Longmans, Green, 1895.   A-H
_____. *Thomas Carlyle: A History of His Life in London,
1834–81.* London, 1884.   A-FH
_____. *Reminiscences of Thomas Carlyle.* 1881.   0-FH
Fullerton, William Morton. *In Cairo.* 1891.   0-FH
_____. *Patriotism and Science.* Boston: Roberts Brothers, 1893.   A-BAR
Funck-Brentano, Frantz. *L'Affaire du collier.* Paris: Hachette,
1901.   A-T
_____. *La Mort de la reine.* 1901.   0-FH
Funk & Wagnall's Standard Dictionary of the English Language.
New York, 1893–95.   0-FH

G

Galsworthy, John. *Plays.* First Series. 1909.   0-FH
Gardiner, Samuel Rawson. *History of England from the
Accession of James I to the Outbreak of the Civil War,
1603–1642.* London: Longman's, Green, 1883–84.   A-H
_____. *History of the Commonwealth and Protectorate.*
1894–1901.   A-FH
_____. *History of the Great Civil War.* 1881–91.   A-FH

Gaskell, Elizabeth. *North and South*. London: Chapman and
Hall, 1855.   A-H

Gauthiez, Pierre. *L'Aretin: 1492–1556*. Paris, 1895.   O-FH

Gautier, Théophile. *Histoire de romantisme*. 1874.   A-FH

_____. *Honoré de Balzac*. Paris: Poulet-Malassis, 1859.   A-BAR

_____. *Mlle de Maupin*. 1871.   A-FH

_____. *Oeuvres: Constantinople*. 1865.   O-FH

_____. *L'Orient*. Paris, 1877.   O-FH

_____. *Premières poésies (1830–45)*. 1870.   O-FH

_____. *Romans et contes*. Paris: Charpentier, 1865.   A-T

_____. *Tableaux de siège, Paris, 1870–1871*. Paris, 1871.   A-BAR

_____. *Les Vacances du lundi*. 1881.   A-FH

Gayley, C. M. *Francis Beaumont*. 1914.   A-FH

Georgian Poetry, 1911–12. 1914 [See also Marsh, Edward].   A-FH

Gibbon, Edward. *The History of the Decline and Fall of the
Roman Empire*. London: John Murray, 1887.   A-FH

_____. *Private Letters of Edward Gibbon*. London: John
Murray, 1896.   A-H

Gissing, George. *By the Ionian Sea*. 1901.   A-FH

_____. *In the Year of Jubilee*. 1895.   O-FH

_____. *New Grub Street*. London: Smith, Elder and Co., 1891.   A-L

Godkin, Edward Lawrence. *Life and Letters*. Ed. Rollo Ogden.
New York: Macmillan, 1907.   A-BAR

_____. *Reflections and Comments (1865–95)*. 1898.   O-FH

_____. *Unforeseen Tendencies of Democracy*. London: Archibald
Constable, 1898.   A-H

Godkin, G. S. *The Monastery of San Marco*. London: Dent,
1901.   A-BAR

Goethe, Johann Wolfgang von. *Autobiography*. London: Bohn's
Library, 1864–66.   O-FH

_____. *Wilhelm Meister's Apprenticeship*. Boston, 1865.   A-FH

_____. *Über Allen Gipfeln*. Munich: Wilhelm Langewiesche-
Brandt, 1908.   O-H

Gogol, Nikolai Vasil'evich. *Les Ames mortes*. Paris: Librairie
Hachette, 1885.   A-H

_____. *Tarass Boulba*. Paris: Hachette, 1874.   A-FH

Goldsmith, Oliver. *She Stoops to Conquer*. Illus. Edwin A.
Abbey. New York: Harper & Brothers, 1887.   O-L

Gomme, Sir Lawrence. *London*. 1914.   A-FH

_____. *The Making of London*. Oxford, 1912.   A-FH

Goncourt, Edmond de. *Chérie*. 1884.   O-FH

_____. *La Faustin*. 1882.   O-FH

———. *La Fille Elisa.* 1882.   0-FH

———. *Les Frères Zéméganno.* 1879.   0-FH

———. *Germinie Lacerteux.* Paris: Alphonse Lemerre, 1876.   A-H

———. *Mlle Clairon.* 1890.   0-FH

Goncourt, Edmond de et Jules de. *Journal (1851–95).* Paris:
G. Charpentier, 1887–96.   0-FH

———. *Oeuvres historiques, romans, etc.* Paris: G. Charpentier,
1876–82.   0-FH

Goncourt, Jules de. *Lettres.* 1885.   0-FH

Gondinet, E. *Théâtre complet.* Paris: C. Lévy, 1892–94.   0-FH

Goodwin, William. *His Friends and Contemporaries.* 1896.   0-FH

Gosse, Sir Edmund. *Biographical Notes on the Writings of
Robert Louis Stevenson.* London: Privately printed at the
Chiswick Press, 1908.   0-H

———. *The Collected Poems of Edmund Gosse.* London:
William Heinemann, 1911.   A-L

———. *Coventry Patmore.* 1905.   0-FH

———. *Critical Kit-Kats.* 1896.   0-FH

———. *Father and Son.* London: William Heinemann, 1907.   A-H

———. *Firdausi in Exile.* 1886.   0-FH

———. *French Profiles.* London: William Heinemann, 1905.   A-L

———. *From Shakespeare to Pope.* Cambridge, 1885.   0-FH

———. *Gossip in a Library.* London: William Heinemann, 1891.   A-L

———. *History of Eighteenth Century Literature.* Macmillan,
1889.   0-FH

———. *Hypolympia.* 1905.   0-FH

———. *Ibsen.* 1907.   0-FH

———. *In Russet and Silver.* 1894.   0-FH

———. *The Jacobean Poets.* London: J. Murray, 1894.   0-FH

———. *Jeremy Taylor.* 1904.   0-FH

———. *King Erik.* 1893.   0-FH

———. *Life and Letters of John Donne.* 1899.   A-FH

———. *Life of Congreve.* London, 1888.   0-FH

———. *Life of Philip Henry Gosse F.R.S.* London: Kegan Paul,
Trench, Trubner, 1890.   A-H

———. *Life of Swinburne.* 1912.   0-FH

———. *Portraits and Sketches.* London: William Heinemann,
1912.   A-L

———. *Questions at Issue.* 1893.   0-FH

———. *Raleigh.* 1886.   0-FH

———. *Seventeenth Century Studies.* 1883.   A-FH

———. *A Short History of Modern English Literature.* London:
Heinemann, 1898.   A-B

_____. *Two Visits to Denmark*. London, 1911.   A-FH

Gozlan, Léon. *Balzac chez lui*. 1863.   0-FH

_____. *Balzac en pantoufles*. Paris, 1865.   A-BAR

Gozzi, Count Carlo. *The Memoirs of Count Carlo Gozzi*.
London: John C. Nimmo, 1890.   A-BAR

Grant, Ulysses Simpson. *Personal Memoirs of U. S. Grant*.
London: Sampson, Low, Marston, Searle, & Rivington,
1885–86.   A-H

Gray, John Alfred. *At the Court of the Amir*. London: Richard
Bentley and Son, 1895.   A-BAR

Gray, Thomas. *The Works of Thomas Gray*. London: William
Pickering [1835]–43.   A-H

_____. *Works*. Ed. E. Gosse. 1884.   A-FH

Green, Alice Stopford. *Irish Nationality*. London: Williams and
Norgate, 1912.   A-BAR

_____. *The Making of Ireland*. 1909.   A-FH

Green, J. R. *The Conquest of England*. London: Macmillan,
1883.   A-H

_____. *Historical Studies*. 1903.   A-FH

_____. *History of the English People*. 1878–80.   A-T

_____. *Letters*. 1901.   A-FH

_____. *The Making of England*. London: Macmillan, 1885.   A-H

_____. *Oxford Studies*. 1901.   A-FH

_____. *Stray Studies from England and Italy*. London:
Macmillan, 1898.   A-H

_____. *Stray Studies*. Second Series. 1903.   A-FH

_____. *Town Life in the Fifteenth Century*. 1894.   A-FH

Gregorovius, Ferdinand. *The Emperor Hadrian*. London:
Macmillan, 1898.   A-H

_____. *Lucrezia Borgia*. Florence: Le Mornier, 1885.   0-FH

_____. *Promenades en Italie*. Paris: Hachette, 1894.   A-FH

Gregory, Sir William. *An Autobiography*. London: John Murray,
1894.   A-BAR

Greville, Charles Cavendish Fulke. *The Memoirs: Reign of
Queen Victoria (1837–52)*. Ed. Henry Reeve. 1885–87.   A-FH

Guérard, E. *Dictionnaire d'anecdotes*. Paris: F. Didot, 1872.   A-FH

Guizot, F. P. G. *Histoire de la civilisation en Europe*. Paris:
Pichon et Didier, 1828.   0-FH

_____. *Histoire de la civilisation en France*. Paris: Pichon et
Didier, 1829.   0-FH

_____. *Histoire de la révolution d'Angleterre*. Paris:
Didier, 1841.   0-FH

Gurney, Edmund. *Phantasms of the Living: Frederic W. H.
Myers, and Frank Podmore.* London: Rooms of the Society for
Psychical Research, Trubner and Company, 1886.   A-BAR
Gyp [Marie-Antoinette de Riquetti de Mirabeau, Comtesse de
Martel de Janville]. *Autour du divorce.* Paris: Calmann
Lévy, 1897.   0-FH
_____. *Autour du mariage.* Paris: Calmann Lévy, 1895.   0-FH
_____. *Monsieur le duc.* Paris: Calmann Lévy, 1893.   0-FH
_____. *Petit Bob.* Paris, 1895.   0-FH

H

Hallam, Henry. *Introduction to the Literature of Europe.* London:
John Murray, 1837–39.   A-BAR
Halliwell-Phillips, J. W. *Outlines of the Life of Shakespeare.*
1885.   0-FH
Halsham, J. *Old Standards: South Country Sketches.* 1913.   A-FH
Hamilton, Anthony, Count. *Mémoires de la vie du Comte de
Grammont.* Cologne: Pierre Marteau, 1713.   A-H
_____. *Mémoires du Chevalier de Grammont.* Paris: Librairie
des Bibliophiles, 1876.   A-H
Hammerton, J. A. *George Meredith in Anecdote and Criticism.*
1909.   A-FH
Hardy, Thomas. *The Well-Beloved.* London, 1897.   A-H
_____. *The Woodlanders.* London: Macmillan, 1887.   A-H
_____. *Tess of the D'Urbervilles.* London: James R. Osgood,
McIlvaine, 1892.   A-T
Hare, Augustus, ed. *Life and Letters of Maria Edgeworth.*
London: Arnold, 1894.   A-E
_____. *Walks in London.* 1901.   0-FH
Harland, Henry. *Mademoiselle Miss.* London: Heinemann, 1893.   0-ML
_____. *My Friend Prospero.* 1904.   0-FH
Harrison, Frederic. *Autobiographic Memoirs.* 1911.   A-FH
_____. *Chatham.* London: Macmillan, 1905.   A-H
_____. *Memories and Thoughts.* 1906.   0-FH
_____. *Tennyson, Ruskin, Mill and Other Literary Estimates.*
London: Macmillan, 1899.   0-BAR
_____. *William the Silent.* London: Macmillan, 1897.   A-H
Harrod, Frances. *Mother Earth.* London: William Heinemann,
1902.   A-BAR
Hawthorne, Nathaniel. *The Blithedale Romance.* Boston: Fields,
Osgood, 1870.   A-H

_____. *The Scarlet Letter.* Boston: James R. Osgood, 1871.   A-H
_____. *The Snow-image, and Other Twice-told Tales.* Boston:
Fields, Osgood, 1869.   A-H
_____. *Transformation [The Marble Faun].* Smith, Elder, 1860.   0-FH
Hazlitt, William. *Characters of Shakespeare's Plays.* London:
C. Templeman, 1848.   A-H
_____. *Criticisms on Art.* London: C. Templeman, 1844.   A-H
_____. *Lectures on the Dramatic Literature of the Age of
Elizabeth.* London: John Templeman, 1840.   A-H
_____. *Liber Amoris.* 1823.   0-FH
_____. *Sketches and Essays.* London: John Templeman, 1839.   A-H
Heine, Heinrich. *Correspondance inédite de Henri Heine.* Paris:
Michel Lévy Frères, vol. I (1866); vol. II (1867).   0-BAR
_____. *De l'Allemagne.* Paris: Michel Lévy Frères, 1855.   0-BAR
_____. *Lutèce.* Paris: Michel Lévy Frères, 1855.   0-BAR
_____. *Reisebilder, tableaux de voyage.* Paris, 1856.   0-BAR
Heinemann, William. *The First Step.* 1895.   0-FH
_____. *Summer Moths.* 1898.   0-FH
Henley, William Ernest. *Three Plays by W. E. Henley and R. L.
Stevenson.* London: David Nutt, 1892.   A-H
_____. *Views and Reviews.* 1890.   A-FH
Hennique, Léon. *L'Accident de M. Hébert.* 1884.   0-FH
_____. *La Dévouée.* 1878.   0-FH
Herbert of Cherbury, Edward Herbert. *The Life of Edward Lord
Herbert, of Cherbury. Written by Himself.* Edinburgh: John
Ballantyne; London: John Murray, 1809.   A-H
Herrick, Robert. *Lyrical Poems.* 1877.   0-FH
Hervey, John. *Memoirs of the Reign of George the Second.*
London: John Murray, 1848.   A-H
Hervieu, Paul Ernest. *Connais-toi.* 1909.   A-FH
_____. *La Course du Flambeau.* Paris, 1901.   0-FH
_____. *Le Dédale.* Paris, 1903.   0-FH
_____. *Le Petit Duc.* Paris, 1896.   0-FH
_____. *Théroigne de Méricourt.* Paris, 1902.   0-FH
Hichens, Robert. *Bella Donna.* 1911.   0-FH
Hill, G. B., ed. *Johnsonian Miscellanies.* Oxford: Clarendon,
1897.   A-T
Hogarth, D. G. *Philip and Alexander of Macedon.* 1897.   A-FH
Hogg, Thomas Jefferson. *The Life of Percy Bysshe Shelley.*
London: Edward Moxon, 1858.   A-H
Holcroft, Thomas. *Memoirs.* London: Longmans, Brown, Green
and Longmans, 1852.   A-H

Holloway, W. *History and Antiquities of Rye.* 1847.   A-FH

_____. *History of Romney Marsh.* 1849.   A-FH

Howells, William Dean. *Annie Kilburn.* Edinburgh, 1888.   A-FH

_____. *April Hopes.* New York, 1888.   A-FH

_____. *Between the Dark and the Daylight.* New York:

Harpers, 1907.   0-FH

_____. *Certain Delightful English Towns.* 1906.   0-FH

_____. *A Chance Acquaintance.* Osgood, 1873.   0-FH

_____. *Christmas Every Day.* Harper, 1893.   0-FH

_____. *The Coast of Bohemia.* New York, 1893.   A-FH

_____. *The Daughter of the Storage.* Harper, 1916.   0-FH

_____. *The Day of Their Wedding.* New York, 1896.   A-FH

_____. *A Day's Pleasure.* Osgood, 1886.   0-FH

_____. *Dr. Breen's Practice.* Osgood, 1881.   0-FH

_____. *A Fearful Responsibility.* Osgood, 1881.   0-FH

_____. *Fennel and Rue.* 1908.   0-FH

_____. *A Foregone Conclusion.* Edinburgh: David Douglas,

1884.   0-BAR

_____. *A Foregone Conclusion.* Osgood, 1875.   0-FH

_____. *A Hazard of New Fortunes.* 1890.   0-FH

_____. *Heroines of Fiction.* New York: Harpers, 1901.   0-FH

_____. *Imaginary Interviews.* New York: Harper & Brothers,

1910.   0-L

_____. *Impressions and Experiences.* New York, 1896.   0-FH

_____. *Indian Summer.* Edinburgh, 1886.   A-FH

_____. *Italian Journeys.* Hurd and Houghton, 1867.   0-FH

_____. *The Kentons.* New York: Harpers, 1902.   A-FH

_____. *The Lady of the Aroostook.* Boston, 1879.   A-FH

_____. *The Landlord at Lion's Head.* Edinburgh, 1897.   A-FH

_____. *Leatherwood God.* Century, 1916.   0-FH

_____. *Letters Home.* New York: Harpers, 1903.   A-FH

_____. *Literature and Life: Studies.* New York: Harper &

Brothers, 1902.   0-L

_____. *London Films.* Harper, 1903.   0-FH

_____. *The Minister's Charge.* Edinburgh, 1886.   A-FH

_____. *Miss Ballard's Inspiration.* New York: Harpers, 1905.   0-FH

_____. *A Modern Instance.* Edinburgh, 1882.   A-T

_____. *The Mother and the Father.* Harper, 1909.   0-FH

_____. *New Leaf Mills.* 1913.   0-FH

_____. *The Open-Eyed Conspiracy.* New York, 1897.   A-FH

_____. *A Pair of Patient Lovers.* New York, 1901.   A-FH

_____. *A Parting and a Meeting.* New York, 1896.   A-FH

————. *Questionable Shapes*. New York: Harpers, 1903. A-FH
————. *Ragged Lady*. Harpers, 1899. A-FH
————. *The Register*. Osgood, 1884. 0-FH
————. *Roman Holidays*. 1908. 0-FH
————. *Seen and Unseen at Stratford on Avon*. 1914. 0-FH
————. *Seven English Cities*. 1909. 0-FH
————. *The Shadow of a Dream*. Edinburgh, 1890. A-FH
————. *The Sleepiing Car*. Osgood, 1884. 0-FH
————. *Son of Royal Langrith*. Harpers, 1904. 0-FH
————. *The Story of a Play*. Harpers, 1898. A-FH
————. *Their Silver Wedding Journey*. Harpers, 1900. A-FH
————. *The Undiscovered Country*. Boston, 1880. A-FH
————. *Venetian Life*. Edinburgh: David Douglas, 1883. 0-BAR
————. *Through the Eye of the Needle*. Harpers, 1907. A-FH
————. *A Woman's Reason*. Edinburgh, 1883. A-FH
————. *The World of Chance*. New York, 1893. A-FH
————. *Years of My Youth*. Harpers, 1916. 0-FH
Hubner, Baron de. *Sixte-Quint*. Paris: Hachette, 1882. A-FH
Hudson, W. H. *Afoot in England*. London: Hutchinson, 1909. A-H
————. *Birds in London*. London: Longmans, 1898. A-FH
————. *A Crystal Age*. London, 1906. 0-FH
Hueffer, Ford Madox. *The Fifth Queen Crowned: A Romance*.
    London: Eveleigh Nash, 1908. 0-L
Hugo, Georges. *Souvenirs d'un matelot*. Paris, 1896. A-BAR
Hunt, Leigh. *The Old Court Suburb (Kensington)*. 1855. 0-FH
Hutchinson, Lucy (Apsley). *Memoirs of the Life of Colonel
    Hutchinson . . . 1822*. London: Longman, Hurst, Rees, Orme,
    and Brown, 1822. A-H
Huxley, Thomas Henry. *Lay Sermons, Addresses, and Reviews*.
    New York: Appleton, 1871. 0-T
————. *Man's Place in Nature*. London: Macmillan, 1894. A-H
————. *Method and Results*. London: Macmillan, 1894. A-H
Huysmans, Joris-Karl. *A Rebours*. Paris: G. Charpentier et
    Cie, 1884. A-L
————. *Certains*. Paris: Tresse & Stock, 1889. A-L
————. *En ménage*. Paris: G. Charpentier, 1881. A-L
————. *En rade*. Paris: Tresse & Stock, 1887. A-L
————. *En route*. Paris: Tresse & Stock, 1895. A-L
————. *Là-bas*. Paris: Tresse & Stock, 1893. A-L
————. *Les Soeurs Vatard*. Paris: G. Charpentier, 1879. A-L

I

Ibsen, Henrik. *Emperor and Galilean*. Ed. William Archer.
   London: Walter Scott, 1890.   0-H
_____. *Ghosts; An Enemy of the People; The Wild Duck*.
   London: Walter Scott, 1890.   0-FH
_____. *Hedda Gabler*. Trans. Edmund Gosse. 1891.   0-FH
_____. *Little Eyolf*. Trans. William Archer. 1895.   0-FH
_____. *Peer Gynt*. Trans. William Archer. London: W. Scott,
   n.d.   0-FH
_____. *Rosmersholm; The Lady from the Sea; Hedda Gabler*.
   London: Walter Scott, 1891.   A-H
Irvine, Alexander F. *Report of the Trial of Madeleine Smith*.
   Edinburgh, 1857.   A-T
Irving, Washington. *Life and Letters*. R. Bentley, 1864.   A-FH
_____. *Life and Voyages of Columbus*. London: J. Murray,
   1849.   A-FH
_____. *Washington Irving's Works*. Vols. I, II, III, V, VI.
   London: n.p., 1824–26.   A-L

J

James, Henry (Sr.). *Lectures and Miscellanies*. New York:
   Redfield, Clinton Hall, 1852.   A-BAR
James, William. *Essays in Honor of*. 1908.   0-FH
_____. *The Literary Remains of the Late Henry James*. Boston:
   James R. Osgood, 1884–85.   A-H
_____. *Louis Agassiz*. Cambridge, Mass.: Harvard University
   Press, 1897.   A-H
Jeaffreson, John Cordy. *Lady Hamilton and Lord Nelson*.
   London: Hurst and Blackett, 1888.   A-H
_____. *The Queen of Naples and Lord Nelson*. London: Hurst
   and Blackett, 1889.   A-H
Jefferies, Richard. *Wild Life in a Southern County*. London:
   Smith, Elder, 1889.   A-H
Jennings, L. J. *Field Paths and Green Lanes*. 1878.   A-FH
_____. *Rambles Among the Hills*. 1880.   A-FH
Jesse, John Heneage. *George Selwyn and his Contemporaries*.
   London: Richard Bentley, 1843–44.   A-H

Jewett, Sarah Orne. *Tales of New England.* London: Osgood,
Mcllvaine, 1893.   0-E
———. *A White Heron and Other Stories.* Boston and New
York: Houghton Mifflin, 1895.   A-BAR
Jewsbury, Miss G. E. *Letters to Jane Welsh Carlyle.* 1892.   A-FH
Johnson, Samuel. *Dictionary of the English Language.* R. G.
Latham, 1866–70.   0-FH
———. *Lives of the Poets.* London, 1896.   0-FH
Johnston, A. S. *Camping Among Cannibals.* London, 1883.   A-FH
Joubert, J. *Les Correspondants.* Paris, 1883.   A-BAR
Jullien, J. *Le Théâtre vivant.* Paris: Charpentier, 1892.   0-FH
Jusserand, Jean Jules. *Les Anglais au moyen âge.* Paris: Librairie
Hachette, 1893.   A-H
———. *The English Novel in the Time of Shakespeare.* 1890.   0-FH
———. *A French Ambassador (at the Court of Charles II).*
1892.   A-FH
———. *Histoire littéraire du peuple anglais.* Paris: Librairie de
Firmin-Didot, 1894.   A-H
———. *Piers Plowman.* 1894.   A-FH
———. *Le Roman d'un roi d'Ecosse.* Paris: Hachette, 1895.   A-FH
Juvenal. *D. Junii Juvenalis et Auli Persii Flacci Styrae.*
Cambridge: G. Thurlbourn and J. Woodyer, 1763.   A-H

K

Karénine, Mme. Wladimir. *George Sand, sa vie et ses oeuvres.*
Paris, 1899–1912.   A-BAR
Keary, C. F. *The Two Lancrofts.* London: Osgood, Mcllvaine and
Company, 1894.   A-BAR
Keats, John. *Letters.* Ed. by S. Colvin. 1891.   0-FH
———. *Life, Letters and Literary Remains of John Keats.* Ed.
Lord Houghton. London: Edward Moxon, 1848.   A-FH
———. *The Works of John Keats.* Ed. H. Buxton Forman.
London, 1883.   A-FH
Kemble, Frances Anne [see also Butler]. *Far Away and Long
Ago.* 1889.   A-FH
———. *Journal of a Residence on a Georgian Plantation
(1838–39).* London: Longman, Green, Longman, Roberts &
Green, 1863.   A-H
———. *Notes upon Some of Shakespeare's Plays.* London:
Richard Bentley, 1882.   A-H

————. *Plays*. London: Longman, 1863.   A-FH
————. *Poems*. 1866.   A-FH
————. *A Year of Consolation*. London: Edward Moxon, 1847.   A-H
Kent-Smith, Charles. *Antiquities of Richborough, Reculver and
Lynne*. 1850.   A-FH
Kenyon, F. G. *Robert Browning and Alfred Domett*. 1906.   0-FH
King, Clarence. *Memoirs*. New York and London: G. P.
Putnam's Sons, 1904.   A-BAR
Kinsley, Charles. *Westward Ho!*. London: Macmillan and Co.,
1881.   A-BAN
Kipling, Rudyard. *Actions and Reactions*. New York: Charles
Scribner's Sons, 1909.   0-H
————. *Captains Courageous*. London and New York:
Macmillan, 1897.   A-H
————. *Captains Courageous*. New York: Scribner's, 1898.   0-H
————. *The Day's Work*. New York: Scribner's, 1899.   0-H
————. *Early Verse*. New York: Scribner's, 1900.   0-H
————. *From Sea to Sea*. New York: Doubleday.   0-FH
————. *The Five Nations*. London: Methuen, 1903.   A-H
————. *The Five Nations*. New York: Scribner's, 1903.   0-H
————. *In Black and White*. New York: Scribner's, 1897.   A-H
————. *The Jungle Book*. New York: Scribner's, 1897.   A-H
————. *Just So Stories for Little Children*. New York:
Scribner's, 1903.   0-H
————. *Kim*. New York: Scribner's, 1902.   0-H
————. *The Light that Failed*. New York: Scribner's, 1897.   A-H
————. *Many Inventions*. 1893.   0-FH
————. *The Naulahka, a Story of West and East*. By Rudyard
Kipling and Wolcott Balestier. London: William
Heinemann, 1892.   0-FH
————. *The Phantom Rickshaw and Other Stories*. New York:
Scribner's, 1897.   A-H
————. *Plain Tales from the Hills*. New York: Scribner's, 1897.   A-H
————. *Puck of Pook's Hill*. New York: Scribner's, 1906.   0-H
————. *Rewards and Fairies*. New York: Scribner's, 1910.   0-H
————. *The Second Jungle Book*. New York: Scribner's, 1897.   A-H
————. *The Seven Seas*. London: Methuen and Co., 1896.   0-L
————. *Soldiers Three, and Military Tales*. New York:
Scribner's, 1897.   A-H
————. *Stalky and Co*. New York: Scribner's, 1900.   0-H
————. *Traffics and Discoveries*. New York: Scribner's, 1904.   0-H
————. *Under the Deodars, The Story of the Gadsbys, Wee
Willie Winkie*. New York: Scribner's, 1897.   A-H

_____. *Verses, 1889–1896.* New York: Scribner's, 1897.	A-H
_____. *Wee Willie Winkie.* Allahabad: Wheeler, 1888.	A-T
_____. *The Writings in Prose and Verse of Rudyard Kipling.*	
New York: Scribner's, 1897–1910.	0-H
Knight, Charles. *Passages of a Working Life.* 1853.	0-FH

L

Labiche, E. *Théâtre complet.* Paris: C. Lévy, 1878–83.	0-FH
Lamb, Charles. *Detached Thoughts on Books.* Norwood,	
U.S.A., 1910.	0-FH
_____. *Letters.* 1888.	0-FH
_____. *Specimens of English Dramatic Poets.* 1854.	A-FH
Landon, F. *Lhasa.* 1905.	A-FH
Lane, Edward William. *The Thousand and One Nights.* London:	
Charles Knight, 1839–41.	A-H
Lanfrey, Pierre. *Correspondance.* Paris: Charpentier, 1885.	0-T
_____. *Histoire de Napoléon Ier.* Paris, n.d.	A-BAR
_____. *Histoire politique des papes.* Paris: Charpentier, n.d.	A-T
Lang, Andrew. *Alfred Tennyson.* 1901.	0-FH
_____. *Ballads and Lyrics of Old France.* 1872.	0-FH
_____. *The Companions of Pickle.* London: Longmans,	
Green, 1898.	A-H
_____. *Custom and Myth.* 1884.	A-FH
_____. *Essays in Little.* 1891.	0-FH
_____. *Helen of Troy.* London: George Bell, 1882.	A-BAR
_____. *History of Scotland.* 1900–1907.	A-FH
_____. *James VI and the Gowrie Mystery.* London: Longmans,	
Green, 1902.	A-H
_____. *Letters on Literature.* London: Longmans, Green and	
Co., 1889.	A-L
_____. *Letters to Dead Authors.* 1886.	0-FH
_____. *The Library.* 1881.	0-FH
_____. *The Life and Letters of John Gibson Lockhart.* London:	
John C. Nimmo; New York: Scribner's, 1896.	A-H
_____. *Lost Leaders.* London: Kegan Paul, Trench and	
Co., 1889.	A-H
_____. *The Mark of Cain.* Bristol, 1886.	A-FH
_____. *A Monk of Fife.* London: Longmans, Green and	
Co., 1896.	A-L
_____. *The Mystery of Mary Stuart.* London: Longmans,	
Green, 1901.	A-H

————. *Myth, Ritual, and Religion.* 1887.   A-FH
————. *Old Friends.* 1890.   A-FH
————. *Pickle, the Spy.* London: Longmans, Green, 1897.   A-FH
————. *Portraits and Jewels of Mary Stuart.* Glasgow, 1906.   0-FH
————. *Prince Prigio.* 1889.   0-FH
————. *Theocritus, Bion, and Moschus rendered into English
Verse.* 1880.   0-FH
————. *The Valet's Tragedy, and Other Studies.* London:
Longmans, Green, 1903.   A-H
Larroumet, Gustave. *Nouvelles Etudes d'histoire et de critique
dramatiques.* Paris, 1899.   A-BAR
Laugel, Auguste. *La France politique et sociale.* Baillière, 1877.   0-FH
————. *Grandes Figures historiques.* Paris: Michel Lévy Frères,
1875.   A-BAR
Lavedan, Henri. *Le Marquis de Priola.* Paris: Ernest
Flammarion, n.d..   0-BAR
Le Gallienne, R. *George Meredith.* 1890   A-FH
Le Sage, R. *Histoire de Gil Blas.* Routledge, n.d.   A-FH
————. *Histoire de Gil Blas.* Paris: Garnier, n.d.   A-FH
————. *Oeuvres choisies.* Paris: Leblanc, 1810.   0-FH
Les Entretiens d'Ariste et D'Eugène. Paris: Sebastien Mabre-
Cramoisy, 1683.   A-BAR
Lecky, W. E. H. *History of England.* 1879–82,   A-FH
Lee, Sir Sidney. *A Life of William Shakespeare.* London: Smith,
Elder, 1898.   A-H
Lemaître, Jules. *Les Rois.* Paris: Calmann Lévy, 1893.   A-BAR
Lenôtre, Gabriel. *La Fille de Louis XVI.* Paris: Perrin et
Cie, 1907   A-BAR
————. *Les Fils de Philippe-égalité.* Paris, 1907.   A-FH
————. *Les Massacres de septembre.* Perrin et Cie, 1907.   0-BAR
————. *Les Noyades de Nantes.* Perrin et Cie, 1912.   0-BAR
Leopardi, Giacomo. *Epistolario de Prospero Vinni.* Florence,
1849.   A-FH
————. *Opere.* Florence, 1865–80.   0-FH
————. *Opere.* Florence, 1907.   0-FH
————. *Le Operette Morali di Giacomo Leopardi.* Livorno,
1870.   A-L
————. *Le Poesie di Jacomo Leopardi.* Livorno, 1869.   A-T
L'Espinasse, Mademoiselle de. *Lettres (1773–1776).* Paris, 1815.   A-FH
Lévy, Arthur. *Napoléon intime.* Paris: E. Plon, 1893.   A-BAR
Lewes, G. H. *Aristotle.* 1864.   A-FH
————. *Life of Goethe.* 1875.   A-FH

Lewis, Caroline. *Clara in Blunderland.* London: Heinemann,
1902.   A-BAR

Linguet, Simon Nicolas Henri. *Mémoires sur la Bastille.* Paris:
Librairie des Bibliophiles, 1889.   A-H

Locke, W. J. *The Kingdom of Theophilus.* 1907.   0-FH

Locker-Lampson, Frederick. *My Confidences.* London: Smith,
Elder & Company, 1896.   A-BAR

Lockhart, J. G. *Peter's Letters to his Kinsfolk.* Edinburgh:
William Blackwood, 1819.   A-BAR

Lodge, H. C. *Early Memories.* New York, 1913.   0-FH

Loftie, W. J. *A History of London.* London: Edward Stanford,
1883.   A-BAR

Loti, Pierre. *Aziyadé.* Paris: Calmann Lévy, 1885.   A-T

———. *Le Chateau de la belle-au-bois-dormant.* Paris:
Calmann Lévy, 1899.   0-T

———. *Les Derniers jours de Pékin.* Paris: Calmann Lévy,
1900.   0-T

———. *Les Désenchantées.* Paris: Calmann Lévy, 1905.   A-T

———. *Le Désert.* Paris, 1895.   0-FH

———. *L'Exilée.* Paris: Calmann Lévy, 1893.   A-T

———. *Fantôme d'Orient.* Paris: Calmann Lévy, 1892.   0-T

———. *Figures et choses qui passaient.* Paris, 1898.   0-FH

———. *Fleurs d'ennui.* Paris: Calmann Lévy, 1883.   0-T

———. *La Galilée.* Paris: Charpentier, 1896.   A-T

———. *Japonneries d'automne.* Paris: Calmann Lévy, 1889.   A-T

———. *Jérusalem.* Paris: Calmann Lévy, 1895.   0-T

———. *Le Livre de la pitié et de la mort.* Paris: Calmann Lévy,
1891.   0-T

———. *Matelot.* Paris: Lemerre, 1893.   A-T

———. *Mon frère Yves.* Paris: Charpentier, 1883.   A-T

———. *La Mort de Philae.* Paris: Calmann Lévy, 1909.   0-T

———. *Pêcheur d'Islande.* Paris: Calmann Lévy, 1886.   A-T

———. *Un Pèlerin d'Angkor.* Paris: Calmann Lévy, 1912.   0-T

———. *Propos d'exil.* Paris: Calmann Lévy, 1887.   0-T

———. *Ramuntcho.* Paris: Calmann Lévy, 1896.   0-T

———. *Reflets sur la sombre route.* Paris, 1899.   0-FH

———. *Le Roman d'un Spahi.* Paris: Calmann Lévy, n.d.   0-T

———. *Le Roman d'un enfant.* Paris: Calmann Lévy, 1892.   0-T

———. *La Troisième jeunesse de Madame Prune.* Paris:
Calmann Lévy, 1900.   0-T

———. *Turquie agonisante.* Paris: Calmann Lévy, 1913.   A-T

———. *Vers Ispahan.* Paris: Calmann Lévy, n.d.   A-T

Louvenjoul, Charles de. *Histoire des oeuvres de Honoré de*
   Balzac. Paris: Calmann Lévy, 1879.   A-T
Lovenjoul, Vicomte Spoelbergh de. *Autour de Honoré de Balzac*.
   Paris: Calmann Lévy, 1897.   0-BAR
Louvet de Couvrai, Jean Baptiste. *Mémoires de Louvet de*
   Couvrai sur la révolution française. Paris: Librairie des
   Bibliophiles, 1889.   A-H
Lowell, James Russell. *Democracy, and Other Addresses*. Boston:
   Houghton Mifflin, 1887 [1886].   0-H
_____. *Heartsease and Rue*. Boston: Houghton Mifflin, 1888.   A-H
_____. *The Writings of James Russell Lowell*. Boston and New
   York: Houghton Mifflin, 1891.   A-BAR
Lowell, Percival. *Mars*. London: Longmans, Green, 1896.   A-BAR
Lucas, E. V. *Charles Lamb and the Lloyds*. Smith, Elder, 1898.   0-FH
Lyall, Sir A. C. *Asiatic Studies*. First Series. 1884.   A-FH
Lytton, Lord [See Bulwer-Lytton]. *What Will He Do with It?*
   1853.   A-FH

M

Macdonald, Maréchal. *Souvenirs*. Paris: E. Plon, 1892.   A-BAR
MacKail, J. W. *Life of William Morris*. 1899.   A-FH
Mackenzie, C. *Carnival*. 1912.   A-FH
_____. *Sinister Street*. 1913.   A-FH
Macready's Reminiscences, etc. New York: Macmillan, 1875.   0-FH
Mahaffy, J. P. *Greek Life and Thought*. 1887.   A-FH
_____. *Greek World under Roman Sway*. 1890.   A-FH
_____. *Social Life in Greece*. 1874.   A-FH
Mahan, Alfred Thayer. *The Life of Nelson*. London: Sampson
   Low, Marston, 1897.   A-H
Main, D. M. *Treasury of English Sonnets*. W. Blackwood, 1880.   0-FH
Maitland, Frederic William. *The Life and Letters of Leslie*
   Stephen. London: Duckworth, 1906.   A-H
Mallarmé, Stéphane. *Vers et prose*. Paris, 1893.   0-FH
Mallock, W. H. *The New Republic*. 1878.   0-FH
Marbot, Général de. *Mémoires*. Paris: E. Plon, 1892.   A-BAR
Marks, John George. *Life and Letters of Frederick Walker*.
   London: Macmillan, 1896.   A-BAR
Marlowe, Christopher. *Works*. London: W. Pickering, 1850.   A-FH
Marsh, Edward, ed. *Georgian Peotry, 1913-1915*. London: The
   Poetry Bookshop, 1915.   A-BAR

Masson, Frédéric. *Napoléon chez lui*. Paris: E. Dentu, n.d.   A-BAR
———. *Napoléon et les femmes*. Paris: Paul Ollendorff, 1894.   A-BAR
Maugras, Gaston. *Les Demoiselles de Verrières*. Paris: Calmann
   Lévy, 1890.   A-BAR
Maupassant, Guy de. *Au Soleil*. 1884.   0-FH
———. *Bel-ami*. Paris: Victor-Havard, 1885.   A-BAR
———. *Clair de lune*. 1888.   0-FH
———. *Contes de la Bécasse*. Paris: Ed. Rouveyre et B. Blond,
   1883.   A-BAR
———. *Des vers*. Paris: Victor-Havard, 1884.   A-FH
———. *L'Inutile Beauté*. 1890.   0-FH
———. *Mlle Fifi*. 1883.   0-FH
———. *Miss Harriet*. Paris: Victor-Havard, 1884.   A-BAR
———. *Oeuvres complètes de Guy de Maupassant: Boule de
   suif*. Paris: Louis Conard, 1908.   A-L
———. *Oeuvres: La Maison Tellier*. Paris: Havard, 1882.   A-T
———. *Sur l'eau*. Marpon, n.d.   A-FH
———. *Une Vie*. Paris: Victor-Havard, 1883.   A-BAR
———. *La Vie errante*. Paris: Paul Ollendorff, 1890.   A-BAR
———. *Yvette*. Paris: Victor-Havard, 1885.   A-BAR
Maxwell, Sir Herbert Eustace. *The Life of Wellington*. London:
   Sampson Low, Marston, 1900.   A-H
Mazade, Charles de. *Le Comte de Cavour*. Paris: E. Plon, 1877.   A-H
McLennan, John Ferguson. *Studies in Ancient History comprising
   a reprint of Primitive Marriage*. London and New York:
   Macmillan and Company, 1886.   A-BAR
Medwin, T. *Life of Percy Bysshe Shelley*. 1847.   0-FH
Meredith, George. *The Adventures of Harry Richmond*. London:
   Smith, Elder & Co., 1871.   A-H
———. *The Amazing Marriage*. Westminster: Archibald
   Constable, 1895.   A-H
———. *Ballads and Poems of Tragic Life*. London: Macmillan,
   1887.   0-H
———. *Beauchamp's Career*. London: Chapman and Hall, 1876.   A-H
———. *Diana of the Crossways*. London: Chapman and Hall,
   1885.   A-H
———. *The Egoist*. London: C. Kegan Paul, 1879.   A-H
———. *Farina*. London: Smith, Elder & Co., 1857.   A-H
———. *Letters of George Meredith*. London: Constable and
   Company, 1912.   A-L
———. *Lord Ormont and His Aminta*. London: Chapman and
   Hall, 1894.   A-H

_____. *One of Our Conquerors.* London: Chapman and
Hall, 1891.   A-H

_____. *The Ordeal of Richard Feverel.* London: Chapman and
Hall, 1859.   A-H

_____. *A Reading of Life.* Westminster: Archibald Constable,
1901.   A-H

_____. *Rhoda Fleming.* London: Tinsley Brothers, 1865.   A-H

_____. *Selected Poems.* London: Archibald Constable, 1897.   A-H

_____. *The Works of George Meredith.* Westminster: Archibald
Constable, 1897.   A-BAR

Mérimée, Prosper. *Colomba.* 1862.   A-FH

_____. *Une Correspondance inédite.* Paris: Calmann Lévy,
1897.   A-BAR

_____. *Lettres à une inconnue.* Paris: Michel Lévy Frères,
1874.   A-BAR

Michelet, Jules. *Richelieu et la Fronde.* Paris: Calmann Lévy,
1899.   A-BAR

Mill, John Stuart. *Dissertations and Discussions: Political,
Philosophical.* Boston: Spencer, 1868.   0-T

Milman, Henry Hart. *Annals of St. Paul's Cathedral.* London:
John Murray, 1868.   A-BAR

_____. *History of Latin Christianity.* 1867.   A-FH

Milton, John. *Minor Poems.* London: printed for C. G. J. and
J. Robinson, 1791.   A-FH

_____. *Works in Verse and Prose.* London: W. Pickering, 1851. 0-FH

Mitchell, L. E. *Poems.* Boston: Houghton Mifflin, 1894.   0-FH

Molière. *Oeuvres.* Paris: Firmin Didot, 1883.   0-FH

Montaigne, Michel de. *Essais de Michel de Montaigne.* Paris:
Garnier Frères, 1865.   A-T

Montégut, Emile. *Souvenirs de Bourgogne.* Paris: Hachette, 1874. 0-FH

Montesquieu [M. de Fezenac]. *Journal de la campagne de
Russie en 1812.* Tours, 1849.   A-FH

Morier, Sir J. *The Adventure of Hajji Baba.* London: Bentley,
1851.   A-T

Morley, John. *Indian Speeches.* 1909.   0-FH

_____. *The Life of William Ewart Gladstone.* London:
Macmillan, 1903.   A-H

_____. *Memoirs of Bartholomew Fair.* London, 1859.   A-FH

_____. *Notes on Politics and History.* London: Macmillan, 1913.   0-H

_____. *Oliver Cromwell.* London: Macmillan, 1900.   A-H

_____. *Rousseau.* London: Chapman and Hall; New York:
D. Appleton and Co., 1873.   A-H

———. *Voltaire.* 1872.	A-HL
———. *Walpole.* London: Macmillan, 1889.	A-BAR
Morris, Newbray. *Montrose.* London: Macmillan, 1892.	A-BAR
Morris, Peter. *Peter's Letters to His Kinsfolk.* 1819.	A-FH
Morris, William. *The Earthly Paradise, a poem.* Boston: Roberts Brothers. Part 1, 1868; Part 3, 1870; Part 4, 1871.	A-BAN
Morse, J. T. *Life and Letters of Oliver Wendell Holmes.* S. Low, 1896.	0-FH
Munthe, Axel. *Memories and Vagaries.* London: Murray, 1908.	A-T
Murray, Gilbert. *Four Stages of Greek Religion.* New York: Columbia, 1912.	A-H
———. *A History of Ancient Greek Literature.* London: William Heinemann, 1897.	A-L
———. *The Stoic Philosophy.* 1915.	A-FH
Musset, Alfred de. *Contes.* Paris, n.d.	0-FH
———. *Comédies.* Paris: Charpentier, 1866.	A-FH
Myers, F. W. H. *Essays—Classical and Modern.* London: Macmillan, 1883.	A-BAR
———. *Wordsworth.* 1881.	A-FH

N

Napier, Sir W. *English Battles and Sieges in the Peninsula.* 1852.	0-FH
New Numbers. Ryton, Dymock, Gloucester. Volume 1, number 4 (December 1914). A quarterly publication of the poems of John Drinkwater, Rupert Brooke, Lascelles Abercrombie, Wilfrid Wilson Gibson.	A-BAN
Newdegate-Newdegate, Lady. *Cavalier and Puritan in the Days of the Stuarts.* London: Smith, Elder & Company, 1901.	A-BAR
Nicolay and Hay. *Abraham Lincoln.* New York, 1890.	A-FH
Nietzsche, Friedrich. *Considération inactuelle.* Paris, 1907.	0-FH
Nodier, Charles. *Promenade de Dieppe aux montagnes d'Ecosse.* Paris: Chez J.N. Barba, 1821.	A-H
Nolhac, Pierre de. *La Reine Marie-Antoinette.* Paris: Alphonse Lemerre, 1892.	A-BAR
Norris, W. E. *Billy Bellew.* New York, 1895.	0-FH
———. *Clarissa Furiosa.* 1897.	0-FH
———. *The Despotic Lady.* 1895.	0-FH
———. *Mrs. Fenton.* 1889.	0-FH
Norton, Charles Eliot. *Historical Studies in Church Building.* New York, 1880.	0-FH

_____. *Letters of Charles Eliot Norton.* London, 1913.   A-FH

Norton, R. *Bernini and Other Studies in the History of Art.* New
York, 1914   0-FH

O

O'Brien, Richard Barry. *The Life of Charles Stewart Parnell,
1846–1891.* London: Smith, Elder & Co., 1898.   A-H

O'Meara, B. E. *Napoleon at St. Helena.* London: Bentley, 1888.   A-BAR

The O'Hara Family; The Bit o' Writin.' Dublin: James Duffy,
1865.   0-T

Ojetti, Ugo. *L'America Vittoriosa.* Milan, 1899.   A-FH

Oliphant, Lawrence. *Picadilly.* 1874.   A-FH

Oliphant, Mrs. M. O. *Autobiography.* 1899.   0-FH

_____. *Miss Majoribanks.* 1866.   0-FH

Oliver, Frederick Scott. *Alexander Hamilton.* London: Archibald
Constable, 1906.   A-H

Orleans, C. d'. *Poésies complètes.* Paris: E. Flammarion, 1876.   0-FH

Orr, Mrs. *Life and Letters of Robert Browning.* 1891.   A-FH

Osbourne, Lloyd. *A Letter to Mr. Stevenson's Friends.* Apia,
Samoa for private circulation, 1894, 1904.   A-H

P

Paget, Violet [Vernon Lee]. *Althea. A Second Book of Dialogues.*
1894.   A-FH

_____. *Ariadne in Mantua.* Oxford, 1903.   0-FH

_____. *Baldwin. A Book of Dialogues.* 1886.   A-FH

_____. *Belcaro (Aesthetical Essays).* 1881.   A-FH

_____. *The Countess of Albany.* 1910.   0-FH

_____. *Euphorion.* 1884.   0-FH

_____. *Genius Loci.* 1899.   0-FH

_____. *Juvenilia.* 1887.   0-FH

_____. *Limbo, and Other Essays.* 1897.   0-FH

_____. *Miss Brown.* 1884.   A-FH

_____. *Poor Jacynth, and Other Tales.* 1904.   0-FH

_____. *Renaissance Fancies and Studies.* 1895.   0-FH

_____. *The Sentimental Traveller.* 1908.   A-FH

_____. *Sister Benvenuta.* 1906.   0-FH

_____. *Studies in the Eighteenth Century in Italy.* 1880.   A-FH

_____. *The Tower of Mirrors.* 1914.   0-FH

Palgrave, W. G. *Central and Eastern Arabia*. 1865.   A-FH
Parkman, Francis. *Montcalm and Wolfe*. London: Macmillan,
1884.   A-FH
Pascal, Blaise. *Les Provinciales*. Paris: G. Charpentier, [ca.
1885?].   A-H
Pater, Walter. *Appreciations: With an Essay on Style*. London:
Macmillan, 1889.   A-L
———. *Essays from The "Guardian"*. London: Printed for
private circulation at the Chiswick Press, 1896.   A-BAR
———. *Gaston de Latour*. London: Macmillan, 1896.   A-L
———. *Greek Studies*. London: Macmillan, 1895.   A-L
———. *Imaginary Portraits*. London: Macmillan, 1887.   A-L
———. *Marius the Epicurean*. 1885.   A-FH
———. *Miscellaneous Studies: A Series of Essays*. London:
Macmillan, 1895.   A-L
———. *Plato and Platonism: A Series of Lectures*. London:
Macmillan, 1893.   A-L
———. *Studies in the History of the Renaissance*. London:
Macmillan, 1873.   A-ML
Patmore, Coventry. *Hastings, Lewes, Rye and the Sussex
Marshes*. 1887.   A-FH
Paton, A. A. *Henry Beyle*. 1874.   A-HL
Pattison, Mark. *Memoirs*. 1885.   0-FH
Peacock, T. L. *Works*. Ed. R. Garnett. Dent, 1891.   A-FH
Pennant, T. *Journey from Chester to London*. 1811.   A-FH
———. *Some Account of London*. 1813.   A-FH
———. *Tours in Wales*. 1810.   A-FH
Pennell, E. R. and J. *Life of J. M. Whistler*. 1909.   0-FH
Pepys, Samuel. *Diary and Correspondence*. London: Bickers and
Son, 1875–79.   A-BAR
———. *The Diary of Samuel Pepys*. London: George Bell,
1893–99.   A-BAR
Perey, Lucien et Maugras, Gaston. *L'Abbé F. Galiani:
correspondance*. Paris: Calmann Lévy, 1881.   A-T
Phelps, W. H. *Words for the Wind*. 1899.   0-FH
Pinero, A. W. *Letty*. 1904.   0-FH
———. *The Princess and the Butterfly*. 1898.   0-FH
Pinks and Wood. *History of Clerkenwell*. 1865.   0-FH
Placci, Carlo. *Un Furto*. Milan, 1892.   0-FH
Plato. *The Dialogues of Plato*. Trans. B. Jowett. Oxford, 1892.   A-FH
Plauchut, Edmond. *Autour de Nohant*. Paris, 1897.   0-FH

Portales, Jean. *Histoire de Martine amoureuse*. Paris, 1912.	O-FH
Prescott, William Hickling. *History of the Reign of Ferdinand and Isabella*. London: Richard Bentley, 1846.	A-H
Prévost, L'Abbé. *Manon Lescaut*. Paris: Quantin, 1879.	A-T
Prévost, Marcel. *Chonchette*. Paris, n.d.	O-FH
———. *Cousine Laura*. Paris, n.d.	O-FH
———. *Les Demi-vièrges*. Paris, 1894.	O-FH
———. *La Fausse Bourgeoise*. Paris: Alphonse Lemerre, 1908.	A-BAR
———. *Frédérique*. Paris, 1900.	O-FH
———. *Léa*. Paris, 1900.	O-FH
———. *Notre campagne*. Paris, 1895.	O-FH
Pouchkine, Alexandre. *Eugène Onéguine*. Paris, 1868.	A-FH

R

Racine, Jean. *Oeuvres*. Paris: Cellot, 1768.	A-T
Rae, Fraser A. *A Biography of Sheridan*. 1896.	A-FH
Raleigh, Walter. *Style*. London and New York: Edward Arnold, 1897.	A-BAR
Raynal, P. de. *Les Correspondants de Joseph Joubert*. 1883.	A-FH
Reade, Charles. *Griffith Gaunt*. London: Chapman and Hall, 1867.	A-BAN
———. *It is Never Too Late to Mend*. London: Richard Bentley, 1856.	A-BAN
Redding, Cyrus. *Fifty Years' Recollections*. 1858.	O-FH
Reid, Forrest. *The Bracknels*. 1911.	O-FH
Rémusat, Charles de. *Abélard*. Paris: Calmann Lévy, 1877.	A-T
———. *Correspondance de M. de Rémusat*. Ed. Paul de Rémusat. Paris: Calmann Lévy, 1883.	A-BAR
———. *Oeuvres—Correspondance, lettres, mémoires*. 1880–81.	A-FH
———. *La Saint-Barthélemy*. Paris: Calmann Lévy, 1878.	A-T
Rémusat, Madame de. *Lettres de Madame Rémusat*. Ed. Paul de Rémusat. Paris: Calmann Lévy, 1881.	A-BAR
———. *Mémoires*. Paris: Calmann Lévy, 1880.	A-BAR
Renan, Ernest. *L'Antéchrist*. Paris, 1873.	O-FH
———. *Conférences d'Angleterre*. Paris, 1880.	O-FH
———. *Dialogues et fragments philosophiques*. Paris, 1876.	A-FH
———. *L'Eglise chrétienne*. Paris: Calmann Lévy, 1879.	A-T
———. *Essais de morale*. Paris: M. Lévy, 1859.	A-FH
———. *Etudes d'histoire religieuse*. Paris: M. Lévy, 1857.	A-FH
———. *Feuilles détachées*. Paris: Calmann Lévy, 1892.	A-T

————. *Histoire du peuple d'Israël*. Paris: Calmann Lévy, 1887.   A-T

————. *Lettres intimes*. Paris: Calmann Lévy, 1896.   A-T

————. *Nouvelles Etudes d'histoire religieuse*. Paris: Calmann
Lévy, 1884.   A-T

————. *Souvenirs d'enfance et de jeunesse*. Paris: Calmann
Lévy, 1883.   A-T

————. *Vie de Jésus*. Paris, 1863.   A-BAR

Richardson, Samuel. *The Works of*. London: Printed for James
Carpenter and William Miller, 1811.   A-BAR

Robertson, George S. *Chitral, The Story of a Minor Siege*.
London: Methuen and Company, 1899.   A-BAR

————. *The Kafirs of the Hindu-Kush*. 1896.   0-FH

Robins, W. *Paddington*. 1853.   0-FH

Rod, Edouard. *Les Grands Ecrivains français: Stendhal*. Paris,
1892.   0-BAR

Rolland, Romain. *Vie de Tolstoi*. Paris: Hachette, 1911.   A-T

Rosebery, Archibald Philip Primrose. *Napoleon, the Last
Phase*. London: Arthur L. Humphreys, 1900.   A-H

Rosny, J. H. *Le Bilatéral*. 1887.   A-FH

————. *Daniel Valgraive*. Paris, 1891.   0-FH

————. *Une reine*. Paris: Plon-Nourrit et Cie, 1901.   A-BAR

Rossetti, Dante Gabriel. *Letters to William Allingham*. Ed.
G. Birkbeck Hill. 1897.   A-FH

Rossetti, William Michael. *Dante Gabriel Rossetti: His
Family-Letters*. London: Ellis and Elvey, 1895.   A-BAR

Rostand, Edmond. *L'Aiglon*. Paris: Charpentier, 1900.   0-FH

————. *Chantecler*. Paris, 1910.   0-FH

Roughead, William, ed. *Trial of Dr. E. W. Pritchard*. 1906.   0-FH

————. *Trial of Mary Blandy*. 1914.   0-T

————. *Twelve Scots Trials*. London: Green, 1913.   0-H

Roux, Emile. *L'Oeuvre médicale de Pasteur*. Monaco, 1906.   0-H

Rutherford, Mark. *Catherine Furze*. London: T. Fisher
Unwin, 1893.   A-BAN

————. *Mark Rutherford's Deliverance: being the second part
of his Autobiography*. Ed. Reuben Shapcott. London:
Trubner, 1885.   A-BAN

S

Saint-Victor, Paul de. *Anciens et modernes*. Paris: Calmann
Lévy, 1886.   A-BAR

_____. *Barbares et bandits.* Paris: Michel Lévy Frères, 1871. A-BAR

_____. *Les Deux masques.* Paris: Calmann Lévy, 1880–84. A-BAR

_____. *Hommes et dieux.* Paris: Michel Lévy Frères, 1867. A-BAR

_____. *Hommes et Dieux.* Paris: M. Lévy, 1880. 0-FH

_____. *Le Théâtre contemporain, Emile Augier, Alexandre Dumas Fils.* Paris, 1889. 0-BAR

_____. *Victor Hugo.* Paris: Calmann Lévy, 1884. A-BAR

Sainte-Beuve, Charles Augustin. *Causeries du lundi.* Paris: Garnier, n.d. 0-FH

_____. *Chateaubriand et son groupe littéraire sous l'empire.* Paris, 1889. 0-FH

_____. *Chroniques parisiennes.* Paris: C. Lévy, 1876. 0-FH

_____. *Correspondance.* Paris: C. Lévy, 1877. 0-FH

_____. *Le Livre d'or de Sainte-Beuve.* 1904. 0-FH

_____. *Nouveaux Lundis.* Paris, 1879. 0-FH

_____. *Nouvelle correspondance.* Paris: C. Lévy, 1880. 0-FH

_____. *P. J. Proudhon.* Paris, 1872. 0-FH

_____. *Port-Royal.* Paris, 1867. 0-FH

_____. *Portraits contemporains.* Paris, 1870. A-FH

_____. *Portraits de femmes.* Paris: Garnier, n.d. 0-FH

_____. *Portraits littéraires.* Paris: Garnier Frères, n.d. 0-FH

Saintsbury, George. *Corrected Impressions.* 1895. A-FH

_____. *Dryden.* 1881. A-FH

_____. *Essays in English Literature, 1780–1860.* London: Percival and Co., 1890. A-L

_____. *Essays on French Novelists.* London: Percival and Co., 1891. A-L

_____. *A History of English Prose Rhythm.* London: Macmillan, 1912. A-H

Sand, George. *André.* Paris: M. Lévy, 1869. 0-FH

_____. *Autour de la table.* E. Jung-Treuttel, n.d. A-BAR

_____. *Correspondance, 1812–76.* Paris: Calmann Lévy. 0-BAN

_____. *Correspondance de George Sand et d'Alfred Musset.* Brussels: Deman, 1904. 0-BAN

_____. *Elle et lui.* Paris: C. Lévy, 1889. 0-FH

_____. *Jacques.* Paris: M. Lévy, 1869. 0-FH

_____. *Mademoiselle La Quintinie.* Paris: Michel Lévy Frères, 1863. A-BAN

_____. *La Piccinino.* Paris: M. Lévy, 1869. 0-FH

_____. *Théâtre complet II.* Paris: Michel Lévy Frères, 1867. A-BAR

_____. *Valentine.* Paris: M. Lévy, 1869. 0-FH

————. *Velvedre.* Paris: C. Lévy, 1861.   0-FH
————. *La Ville noire.* Paris: Michel Lévy Frères, 1861.   A-L
Santayana, George. *Interpretations of Poetry and Religion.*
    1900.   A-FH
————. *The Sense of Beauty.* 1896.   A-FH
————. *Winds of Doctrine.* London: Dent, 1913.   A-H
Sardou, Victorien. *La Sorcière.* Paris, 1904.   0-FH
Schiller, Friedrich von. *Sämmtliche Werke.* Stuttgart, 1879. 0-FH
Schopenhauer, Arthur. *Essays.* Sonnenschein, 1899.   0-FH
Scott, Sir Walter. *Familiar Letters.* Edinburgh, 1894.   A-FH
————. *Journal.* Edinburgh, 1891.   A-FH
————. *Memoirs of the Life of Sir Walter Scott, Bart.*
    Edinburgh: Robert Cadell, 1839.   A-BAN
Scribe, Eugène. *Théâtre.* Paris: A. André, 1828.   0-FH
Serao, Matilde. *Il Paese di Cuccagna.* Milan, 1891.   A-FH
Settembrini, Luigi. *Recordanze della mia Vita.* Naples:
    Antonio Morano, 1879–80.   A-BAR
Seward, A. *Anecdotes of Distinguished Persons.* 1795–97.   0-FH
Shakespeare, William. *Poems, with Notes by G. Wyndham.*
    London: Methuen, 1898.   A-T
————. *Sonnets, with Notes by Samuel Butler.* 1899.   0-FH
————. *Works.* Ed. C. H. Herford. 1899.   0-FH
————. *The Works of William Shakespeare.* Ed. William
    George. Cambridge and London: Macmillan. 1863–66.   A-H
Shaw, George Bernard. *Plays: Pleasant and Unpleasant.*
    Chicago: Herbert S. Stone, 1904.   A-H
Sheppard, Edgar. *Memorials of St. James's Palace.* London:
    Longmans, Green, 1894.   A-BAR
Smith, Charles Roach. *The Antiquities of Richborough,
    Reculver, and Lymne, in Kent.* London: John Russell Smith,
    1850.   A-BAR
Smith, Dr. W. *Dictionary of Greek and Roman Antiquities.*
    1851.   A-FH
————. *New Classsical Dictionary.* 1853.   0-FH
Smith, Logan Pearsall. *The English Language.* London:
    Williams and Norgate, 1912.   A-H
————. *The Youth of Parnassus and Other Stories.* London:
    Macmillan, 1895.   0-L
Smith, Sir Harry. *The Autobiography of Sir Harry Smith.*
    London: John Murray, 1910.   A-H
Smollett, Tobias. *The Adventures of Roderick Random.*
    London: James Cochrane, 1831.   A-H

_____. *The Expedition of Humphry Clinker*. London:
Cochrane and Pickersgill, 1831.   A-H
The Social Circle in Concord, Mass. Cambridge, Mass:
Riverside Press, for the Social Circle in Concord, June
1903. The centenary of the birth of Ralph Waldo Emerson
as observed in Concord, May 25, 1903, under the direction
of the Social Circle.   A-H
Sophocles, *Oedipus*. Trans. Gilbert Murray. New York:
Oxford, 1911.   A-H
Southey, Robert. *Roderick*. 1818.   0-FH
Spencer, Herbert. *An Autobiography*. London: Williams and
Norgate, 1904.   A-T
_____. *Education: Intellectual, Moral and Physical*. New
York: Appleton, 1871.   0-T
_____. *Essays: Moral, Political and Aesthetic*. New York:
Appleton, 1871.   A-T
_____. *Illustrations of Universal Progress*. New York:
Appleton, 1870.   A-T
Spingarn, Joel. *The New Criticism*. New York: Columbia
Univ. Press, 1911.   0-T
Stanley, A. P. *Memorials of Westminster Abbey*. 1868.   A-FH
Stendhal (Henri Beyle). *Oeuvres complètes de Stendhal: Rome,
Naples et Florence*. Paris: Michel Lévy Frères, 1865.   A-L
_____. *Le Rouge et le Noir*. Paris: Michel Lévy Frères,
1870.   A-H
Stephen, Sir James. *Essays in Ecclesiastical Biography*.
London: Longman, Green, Longman, and Roberts, 1860.   A-H
Stephen, Leslie. *An Agnostic's Apology, and Other Essays*.
London: Smith, Elder, 1893.   A-H
_____. *Hours in a Library*. London: Smith, Elder, 1892.   A-H
_____. *The Playgrounds of Europe*. London, 1894.   A-FH
_____. *Social Rights and Duties*. London: Swan
Sonnenschein; New York: Macmillan, 1897.   A-H
_____. *Studies of a Biographer*. London: Duckworth,
1898–1902.   A-H
Sterne, Laurence. *Works*. 1808.   0-FH
Stevenson, Robert Louis. *Across the Plains*. London: Chatto &
Windus, 1892.   A-H
_____. *Ballads*. London: Chatto & Windus, 1890.   A-H
_____. *Catriona*. London: Cassell, 1893.   A-H
_____. *The Ebb-Tide*. London: William Heinemann, 1894.   A-H
_____. *Edinburgh*. London: Seeley & Co., 1889.   A-H

————. *Familiar Studies of Men and Books*. London: Chatto
& Windus, 1882.   A-H

————. *A Footnote to History*. London: Cassell, 1892.   0-H

————. *Island Nights' Entertainments*. London: Cassell, 1893.   A-H

————. *Kidnapped*. London: Cassell, 1886.   0-H

————. *The Letters of Robert Louis Stevenson*. Ed. Sir Sidney
Colvin. London: Methuen, 1911.   A-H

————. *The Master of Ballantrae*. London: Cassell, 1889.   A-H

————. *Memories and Portraits*. London: Chatto & Windus,
1887.   A-H

————. *New Arabian Nights*. London: Chatto & Windus,
1887.   A-H

————. *The Silverado Squatters*. London: Chatto & Windus,
1883.   A-H

————. *St. Ives*. London: William Heinemann, 1898.   A-H

————. *Strange Case of Dr. Jekyll and Mr. Hyde*. London:
Longmans, Green, 1886.   A-H

————. *Treasure Island*. London: Cassell, 1884.   A-H

————. *Underwoods*. London: Chatto & Windus, 1887.   A-H

————. *Vailima Letters,* London: Methuen, 1895.   A-H

————. *Virginibus Puerisque, and Other Papers*. London:
Ç. Kegan Paul, 1881.   0-H

————. *Weir of Hermiston*. London: Chatto and Windus,
1896.   A-H

————. *The Wrecker*. By Robert Louis Stevenson and Lloyd
Osbourne. London: Cassell, 1892.   A-H

Story, William Wetmore. *A Poet's Portfolio: Later Readings*.
Edinburgh and London: William Blackwood and Sons, 1894.   A-BAR

Stow, John. *A Survey of London*. Oxford: Clarendon, 1908.   A-BAR

Strauss, D. F. *Nouvelle Vie de Jésus*. Paris: Librairie
Internationale, 1864.   0-T

Stuart, Lady Louisa. *Some Account of John Duke of Argyll
and His Family*. London: W. Clowes, 1863.   A-H

Sturgis, Julian. *A Book of Song*. 1894.   0-FH

Sturgis, Russell. *From Books and Papers of.* Oxford: 1893.   0-FH

Swift, Jonathan. *Letters*. Ed. J. Hawkesworth.   A-FH

————. *Life*. 1893.   0-FH

————. *The Works of Dr. Jonathan Swift*. Ed. John
Hawkesworth. London: n.p., 1766.   A-L

Swinburne, Algernon Charles. *Atalanta in Calydon*. London:
Chatto & Windus, 1875.   A-H

————. *Bothwell: A Tragedy*. London: Chatto & Windus,
1875.   A-L

_____. *Chastelard: A Tragedy.* London: Chatto & Windus, 1875.   A-L

_____. *Erechtheus.* 1876.   A-FH

_____. *Essays and Studies.* London: Chatto & Windus, 1875.   A-L

_____. *George Chapman: A Critical Essay.* London: Chatto & Windus, 1875.   A-L

_____. *Marino Faliero: A Tragedy.* London: Chatto & Windus, 1875.   A-L

_____. *A Midsummer Holiday and Other Poems.* London: Chatto & Windus, 1884.   A-L

_____. *Miscellanies.* London: Chatto & Windus, 1886.   A-L

_____. *A Study of Ben Jonson.* London: Chatto & Windus, 1889.   A-L

_____. *Tristram of Lyonesse and Other Poems.* London: Chatto & Windus, 1882.   A-L

_____. *Works.* London: George Chapman, 1875–92.   0-FH

Symonds, John Addington. *Animi Figura.* London: Smith, Elder & Company, 1882.   A-BAR

_____. *Blank Verse.* 1895.   A-FH

_____. *Giovanni Boccaccio as Man and Author.* London: John C. Nimmo, 1895.   A-BAR

_____. *Italian Byways.* London: Smith, Elder & Company, 1883.   A-L

_____. *The Life of Benvenuto Cellini.* 1886.   A-FH

_____. *The Life of Michelangelo Buonarrotti.* London: John C. Nimmo, 1892.   A-H

_____. *Many Moods: A Volume of Verse.* London: Smith, Elder & Co., 1878.   0-L

_____. *Memoirs of Count Carlo Gozzi.* 1890.   A-FH

_____. *New and Old.* 1880.   0-FH

_____. *Our Life in the Swiss Highlands.* London and Edinburgh: Adam and Charles Black, 1892.   A-BAR

_____. *Renaissance in Italy: The Age of the Despots.* London: Smith, Elder & Co., 1880.   A-BAR

_____. *Renaissance in Italy: The Catholic Reaction.* London: Smith, Elder & Co., 1886.   A-BAR

_____. *Renaissance in Italy: The Fine Arts.* London: Smith, Elder & Co., 1882.   A-BAR

_____. *Renaissance in Italy: Italian Literature.* London: Smith, Elder & Co., 1881.   A-BAR

_____. *Renaissance in Italy: The Revival of Learning.* London: Smith, Elder & Co., 1882.   A-BAR

————. *Sir Philip Sidney*. 1886.   A-FH
————. *Sketches and Studies in Italy*. 1879.   A-FH
————. *Studies of the Greek Poets*. 1873.   A-FH
————. *Vagabunduli Libellus*. 1884.   A-FH
————. *Walt Whitman*. London: John C. Nimmo, 1893.   A-H

T

Taillandier, Saint-René. *Drames et romans de la vie littéraire.*
    Paris: Librairie des Bibliophiles, 1871.   A-BAR
Taine, Hippolyte. *Carnets de voyage: Notes sur la province,*
    1863–1865. Paris: Librairie Hachette, 1897.   0-L
————. *Derniers essais de critique et d'histoire*. Paris, 1894.   0-FH
————. *La Fontaine et ses fables*. Paris: Librairie Hachette,
    1870.   A-L
————. *Histoire de la littérature anglaise*. Paris: Librairie
    Hachette, 1866.   A-L
————. *Notes sur l'Angleterre*. Paris: Librairie Hachette,
    1872.   A-L
————. *Nouveaux essais de critique et d'histoire*. Paris:
    Hachette, 1901.   0-BL
————. *Origines de la France Contemporaine*. Paris:
    Hachette, 1876–85.   A-T
————. *Sa vie et sa correspondance*. Paris: Librairie
    Hachette, 1902–5.   A-L
————. *Voyage aux Pyrénées*. Paris: Hachette, 1860.   A-H
————. *Voyage en Italie*. Paris: Hachette, 1866.   A-T
Tallement des Réaux. *Les Historiettes*. Paris: J. Techner,
    1854–60.   A-FH
Tardou, V. *La Sorcière*. Paris: C. Lévy, n.d.   0-FH
Tarver, J. C. *Phraseological French Dictionary*. 1845.   0-FH
Taylor, Jeremy. *The Rule and Exercises of Holy Dying.*
    London: Bell and Daldy, 1857.   A-H
Taylor, Tom. *Life of Benjamin Robert Haydon*. London:
    Longmans, Brown, Green, and Longmans, 1853.   A-BAR
Tennyson, Alfred. *Ballads and Other Poems*. 1880.   0-FH
————. *Becket*. 1884.   0-FH
————. *The Death of Oenone and Other Poems*. 1892.   0-FH
————. *Demeter, and Other Poems*. 1889.   0-FH
————. *Life by His Son*. 1897.   0-FH
————. *Maud and Other Poems*. London: Moxon, 1862.   0-BAN

———. *Poems*. London: Edward Moxon, 1857.   A-H
Thackeray, William Makepeace. *The Adventures of Philip on
His Way through the World*. London: Smith, Elder, 1862.   A-BAN
———. *A Collection of Letters of W. M. Thackeray,
1847–1855*. London: Smith, Elder, 1887.   A-H
———. *Denis Duval*. London: Smith, Elder, 1867.   A-BAN
———. *The English Humorists of the Eighteenth Century*.
London: Smith, Elder, 1853.   A-BAN
———. *The Four Georges*. London: Smith, Elder, 1861.   A-BAN
———. *The History of Henry Esmond*. London: Smith, Elder,
1861.   A-BAN
———. *The History of Pendennis*. London: Bradbury &
Evans, 1849, 1850.   A-BAN
———. *The History of Samuel Titmarsh and the Great
Hoggarty Diamond*. London: Bradbury & Evans, 1849.   A-BAN
———. *The Irish Sketch Book by Mr. M. A. Titmarsh*.
London: Chapman and Hall, 1845.   A-BAN
———. *Lovel the Widower*. London: Smith, Elder, 1861.   A-BAN
———. *Miscellanies: Prose and Verse*. London: Smith, Elder,
1866.   A-BAN
———. *The Newcomes*. London: Bradbury & Evans, 1855.   A-BAN
———. *Notes of a Journey from Cornhill to Grand Cairo*.
London: Smith, Elder, 1865.   A-BAN
———. *The Paris Sketch Book: by Mr. Titmarsh*. London:
John Macrone, 1840.   A-H
———. *The Paris Sketch Book*. London: Smith, Elder, 1866.   A-BAN
———. *Roundabout Papers*. London: Smith, Elder, 1863.   A-BAN
———. *Vanity Fair*. London: Bradbury & Evans, 1848.   A-BAN
———. *The Virginians*. London: Bradbury & Evans,
1858–59.   A-BAN
Thanet, Octave. *The Missionary Sheriff*. London: Harper,
1897.   A-BAR
Theocritus. *Specimens of a Translation*. London: Chiswick
Press, n.d.   A-T
Thiebault, Paul. *Mémoires du Général Thiebault*. Paris:
Librairie Plon, 1893–95.   A-H
Thomson, Richard. *Chronicles of London Bridge*. 1827.   0-FH
Tocqueville, Alexis de. *De la démocratie en Amérique*. Paris:
Charles Gosselin et W. Coquebert, 1839–40.   A-BAR
Tolstoi, Léon. *Anna Karénine*. Paris: Librairie Hachette, 1886.   A-T
Topffer, R. *Nouveaux Voyages en Zigzag*. 1854.   0-FH
———. *Voyages en Zigzag*. 1850.   0-FH

Tourguénieff, Ivan [see also under Turgenev]. *Un Bulgare.*
    Paris, 1886.   0-BAR
_____. *Dimitri Roudine.* Paris: J. Hatzel, n.d.   0-BAR
_____. *Les Eaux printanières.* Paris: J. Hetzel, n.d.   0-BAR
_____. *Fumée.* Paris: J. Hetzel et Cie, n.d.   A-BAR
_____. *Une nichée de gentilshommes.* Paris, 1862.   0-BAR
_____. *Nouvelles Moscovites.* Paris, n.d.   0-BAR
_____. *Nouvelles scènes de la vie russe.* Paris, 1887.   0-BAR
_____. *Oeuvres dernières.* Paris, n.d.   0-BAR
_____. *Pères et enfants.* Paris, 1884.   0-BAR
_____. *Scènes de la vie russe.* Paris, 1887.   0-BAR
_____. *Souvenirs d'enfance.* Paris, n.d.   0-BAR
Tozer, Rev. H. F. *English Commentary on Dante's Divina
    Commedia.* Oxford, 1901.   0-FH
Traill, H. D. *The New Lucian.* 1884.   A-FH
Traubel, H. *With Walt Whitman in Camden.* New York, 1908.   0-FH
Trent, W. P. *History of American Literature.* London:
    Heinemann, 1903.   0-FH
Trevelyan, George Macaulay. *England in the Age of Wycliffe.*
    London: Longmans, Green, 1909.   A-H
_____. *Memoir of Theodore Trevelyan.* 1914.   0-FH
Trevelyan, George Otto. *The Early History of Charles James
    Fox.* London: Longmans, Green, 1880.   A-H
_____. *Interludes in Verse and Prose.* London: George Bell
    and Sons, 1905.   A-BAR
Trevelyan, G. W. *The Poetry and Philosophy of George
    Meredith.* 1906.   0-FH
Trevelyan, William. *Trial of Mary Blandy.* London: William
    Hodge, 1914.   A-H
Trewen, A. L. *History of Brickwall in Sussex.* 1909.   0-FH
Trollope, Anthony. *An Autobiography.* [Vol. I only].
    Edinburgh and London: William Blackwood and Sons, 1883.   A-BAN
Trollope, T. A. *Tuscany in 1849–59.* 1859.   0-FH
Turgenev, Ivan Sergeevich [see also under Tourguénieff]. *A
Desperate Character and Other Stories.* London: William
    Heinemann, 1899.   A-H
_____. *The Diary of a Superfluous Man, and Other Stories.*
    London: William Heinemann, 1899.   A-H
_____. *Dream Tales, and Prose Poems.* London: William
    Heinemann, 1897.   A-H
_____. *The Jew, and Other Stories.* London: William
    Heinemann, 1899.   A-H
_____. *Liza, or a Noble Nest.* London: Ward, Lock, n.d.   A-T

————. *A Lear of the Steppes, and Other Stories*. London: William Heinemann, 1898.   A-T

————. *Nouvelles Moscovites*. Paris: J. Hetzel et cie., 1869.   A-H

————. *On the Eve*. London: William Heinemann, 1895.   A-H

————. *Rudin*. London: William Heinemann, 1894.   A-H

————. *Smoke*. London: William Heinemann, 1896.   A-H

————. *The Torrents of Spring*. London: William Heinemann, 1897.   A-H

————. *Virgin Soil*. London: William Heinemann, 1896.   A-H

Twelve English Statesmen—William the Conqueror, Walpole, etc. 1888–93.   A-FH

U

Upward, Allen. *Secret History of To-Day*. 1904.   0-FH

V

Vadier, Berthe. *Henri-Frédéric Amiel*. 1886.   A-FH

Vallès, J. *Jacques Vingtras. Le Bachelier*. 1881.   0-FH

Vasari, C. *Le Vite de Pittori, Scultori, etc*. Florence: F. Le Monnier, 1846–70.   A-FH

Verga, G. *Vagabondaggio*. Florence, 1887.   A-FH

Verney, Frances Parthenope (Nightingale) Lady. *Memoirs of the Verney Family*. London: Longmans, Green, 1892–99.   A-H

Vies des saints . . . selon le bréviaire romain. Paris: Ruffet, 1865.   A-BAR

Vigny, Alfred de. *Servitude et grandeurs militaires*. Paris, 1870.   0-FH

Villari, Pasquale. *Jerome Savonarola et son temps*. Paris, 1874.   0-FH

W

Waliszewski, Kazimierz. *Autour d'un trône: Catherine II de Russie*. Paris: Librairie Plon, 1894.   A-H

————. *History of Russian Literature*. London: Heinemann, 1900.   0-FH

————. *Pierre le Grand*. Paris: Librairie Plon, 1897.   A-H

_____. *Le Roman d'une impératrice: Catherine II de Russie.*
Paris: Librairie Plon, 1893.   A-H
Wallon, H. *Jeanne d'Arc.* Paris, 1875.   0-FH
Walpole, Horace. *The Letters of Horace Walpole.* Ed. Peter
Cunningham. London: Bickers and Son, 1880.   A-BAR
Walpole, Hugh. *The Duchess of Wrexe: Her Decline and
Death.* London: Martin Secker, 1914.   0-L
_____. *Fortitude.* 1913.   0-FH
_____. *Maradick at Forty.* 1910.   0-FH
_____. *The Prelude to Adventure.* 1912.   0-FH
_____. *The Wooden Horse.* London: Smith, Elder & Co.,
1909.   0-L
Warburton, E. *Prince Rupert and the Cavaliers.* 1849.   A-FH
Ward, Mrs. Humphry. *The Case of Richard Meynell.* 1911.   0-FH
_____. *The Coryston Family.* 1913.   A-FH
_____. *Diana Mallory.* London: Smith, Elder & Co., 1908.   A-T
_____. *Eleanor.* 1900.   0-FH
_____. *Helbeck of Bannisdale.* London: Smith, Elder & Co.,
1898.   A-L
_____. *The History of David Grieve.* London: Smith, Elder
& Co., 1892.   A-L
_____. *Lady Rose's Daughter.* 1903.   0-FH
_____. *Marcella.* 1894.   A-FH
_____. *The Marriage of William Ashe.* New York: Harper,
1905.   A-P
_____. *The Mating of Lydia.* 1913.   0-FH
_____. *Robert Elsmere.* Vols. I and II of the Westmoreland
Edition. Boston: Houghton Mifflin, 1911.   A-L
_____. *Sir George Tressady.* 1896.   0-FH
Watson, Rosamund M. *Vespertilia.* 1895.   0-FH
Webb, Honour Judge. *The Mystery of William Shakespeare.*
1902.   A-FH
Wells, H. G. *Anne Veronica.* 1909.   A-FH
_____. *Anticipations.* 1903.   A-FH
_____. *The Discovery of the Future.* London: Fisher, 1902. 0-T
_____. *An Englishman Looks at the World.* 1914.   A-FH
_____. *First and Last Things.* 1908.   0-FH
_____. *The First Men in the Moon.* 1901.   0-T
_____. *The Future in America.* 1906.   A-FH
_____. *In the Days of the Comet.* 1906.   0-FH
_____. *Mankind in the Making.* 1903.   A-FH
_____. *A Modern Utopia.* 1905.   A-FH

_____. *The New Machiavelli.* 1911.   A-FH

_____. *New Worlds for Old.* London: Archibald Constable
and Co., 1908.   A-L

_____. *The Passionate Friends.* 1913.   A-FH

_____. *Tales of Space and Time.* Harper's, 1900.   0-FH

_____. *Tono Bungay.* 1909.   A-FH

_____. *Twelve Stories and a Dream.* 1903.   0-FH

_____. *The World Set Free: A Story of Mankind.* London:
Macmillan, 1914.   0-L

Wendell, Barrett. *A Literary History of America.* London:
T. Fisher Unwin, 1901.   A-H

Wharton, Edith. *Crucial Instances.* 1901.   A-FH

_____. *The Custom of the Country.* New York: Charles
Scribner's Sons, 1913.   A-L

_____. *The Descent of Man and Other Stories.* London:
Macmillan, 1904.   A-L

_____. *Ethan Frome.* Macmillan, 1911.   A-FH

_____. *The Fruit of the Tree.* New York, 1907.   A-FH

_____. *A Gift From the Grave.* London: John Murray, 1901.   A-L

_____. *Italian Backgrounds.* New York: Charles Scribner's
Sons, 1905.   0-L

_____. *A Motor-Flight through France.* New York, 1908.   0-FH

_____. *The Reef: A Novel.* London: Macmillan, 1912.   A-L

_____. *Sanctuary.* London: Macmillan, 1903.   A-L

_____. *Tales of Men and Ghosts.* New York, 1910.   A-FH

Wheatley and Cunningham. *London Past and Present.* 1891.   A-FH

Wheatley, Henry Benjamin. *Hogarth's London.* 1909.   0-FH

_____. *The Story of London.* London: J. M. Dent, 1904.   A-H

Whistler, J. M. *The Gentle Art of Making Enemies.* 1890.   A-FH

Whitman, Walt. *Leaves of Grass.* Philadelphia: McKay, 1900.   A-FH

_____. *The Wound Dresser.* Ed. Richard Maurice Bucke.
Boston: Small, Maynard and Company, 1898.   A-BAR

Wilde, Oscar. *Salomé.* Paris: Librairie de l'Art Indépendant;
London: Elkin Matthew and John Lane, 1893.   A-T

Windham Baring, William. *Diary (1784–1810).* London, 1866.   A-FH

Wister, Owen. *Lady Baltimore.* New York: Macmillan, 1906.   A-H

_____. *The Seven Ages of Washington.* New York:
Macmillan Company, 1907.   0-H

_____. *Ulysses S. Grant.* Boston: Small, Maynard and Co.,
1900.   A-T

Wolseley, Garnet Joseph. *The Decline and Fall of Napoleon.*
London: Sampson Low, Marston, 1895.   A-H

Wolseley, Field-Marshal Viscount. *The Story of a Soldier's Life*. Westminster: Archibald Constable, 1903.   A-BAR

Woodberry, George. *North Africa and the Desert*. New York: Scribner's, 1914.   A-T

Woolson, Constance Fenimore. *Anne*. New York: Harper, ca. 1882.   A-BAR

_____. *For the Major*. New York: Harper, 1883.   0-FH

_____. *The Front Yard and Other Italian Stories*. New York: Harper, 1895.   A-BAR

_____. *Horace Chase*. London: Osgood, McIlvaine, 1894.   A-BAR

_____. *Jupiter Lights*. New York: Harper, 1889.   A-BAR

_____. *Mentone, Cairo, and Corfu*. New York: Harper, 1896.   A-BAR

_____. *Rodman the Keeper: Southern Sketches*. New York: D. Appleton, 1880.   A-BAR

Y

Young, F. *Christopher Columbus and the New World*. 1906.   A-FH

Yriarte, Charles. *Les Borgia*. Paris: Rothschild, 1889.   A-T

Z

Zeller, M. Jules. *Entretiens sur l'histoire: Italie et Renaissance*. Paris: Librairie Académique, 1869.   A-BAR

_____. *Les Tribuns et les révolutions en Italie*. Paris: Didier, 1874.   A-BAR

Zola, Emile. *L'Argent*. Paris: Charpentier, 1891.   0-T

_____. *L'Assommoir*. Paris: Charpentier, 1888.   0-T

_____. *Au Bonheur des dames*. Paris: Charpentier, 1885.   A-T

_____. *La Bête humaine*. Paris: Charpentier, 1890.   0-T

_____. *Une campagne*. Paris: Charpentier, 1882.   0-T

_____. *Le Capitaine Burle*. Paris: Charpentier, 1883.   0-T

_____. *La Conquête de Plassans*. Paris: Charpentier, 1880.   0-T

_____. *La Curée*. Paris: Charpentier, 1880.   0-T

_____. *La Debâcle*. Paris: Charpentier, 1892.   0-T

_____. *Le Docteur Pascal*. Paris: Charpentier, 1893.   0-T

_____. *Documents littéraires*. Paris: Charpentier, 1881.   0-T

_____. *Fécondité*. Paris: Charpentier, 1899.   A-T

_____. *La Fortune des Rougon*. Paris: Charpentier, 1879.   0-T

——. *Germinal*. Paris: Charpentier, 1885.   A-T
——. *La Joie de vivre*. Paris: Charpentier, 1884.   0-T
——. *Lourdes*. Paris: Charpentier, 1894.   0-T
——. *Mes haines*. Paris: G. Charpentier, 1879.   A-BAR
——. *Mes haines*. Paris: Charpentier, 1895.   0-T
——. *Naïs Micoulin*. Paris: Charpentier, 1884.   0-T
——. *Nana*. Paris: Charpentier, 1895.   0-T
——. *Le Naturalisme au théâtre*. Paris: Charpentier, 1881.   0-T
——. *Nos auteurs dramatiques*. Paris: Charpentier, 1881.   0-T
——. *L'Oeuvre*. Paris: Charpentier, 1886.   0-T
——. *Une page d'amour*. Paris: Charpentier, 1878.   0-T
——. *Paris*. Paris: Charpentier, 1898.   A-T
——. *Pot-bouille*. Paris, 1892.   0-FH
——. *Le Rêve*. Paris: Charpentier, 1888.   0-T
——. *Le Roman expérimental*. Paris: Charpentier, 1880.   A-T
——. *Les Romanciers naturalistes*. Paris: Charpentier,
1895.   0-T
——. *Rome*. Paris: Charpentier, 1896.   A-T
——. *Les Soirées de Médan*. Paris: Charpentier, 1880.   0-T
——. *Son excellence Eugène Rougon*. Paris: Charpentier,
1881.   0-T
——. *La Terre*. Paris: Charpentier, 1887.   0-T
——. *Théâtre*. Paris: Charpentier, 1894.   0-T
——. *Travail*. Paris: Charpentier, 1901.   A-T
——. *Le Ventre de Paris*. Paris: Charpentier, 1880.   0-T
——. *Vérité*. Paris: Charpentier, 1903.   A-T

The Books in the Books: What Henry James's Characters Read and Why

Adeline R. Tintner

Henry James read books, wrote books, bought books, presented books, edited books, and wrote prefaces to books. The evidence of their presence in his life and work is reflected in his constant allusion, in novels and tales, to all aspects of book-life and the presence of books in civilized existence. In his work, James uses books in many subtle ways because they were present in the society he pictures. But he draws also on their presence in the life of the literary artist—that is, himself. His library contained many of the authors he mentioned; but he had available to him other libraries—in his early days the Redwood Library in Newport. There had been, even earlier, his father's books, and the magazines the James family subscribed to, when living in their 14th Street house in New York. In mature life he had two club libraries available to him constantly—those of the Athenaeum and the Reform Clubs. Although there is no mention of his using the British Museum library (for as a writer of fiction, James was less interested in research libraries than men like Shaw, preoccupied with social problems and many branches of learning), there are certain kinds of reference books and "useful information" books that appear in his novels. A court guide figures in *The Tragic Muse;* Bradshaw is used in "A London Life." The *New York Directory* (fig. 2), that fascinating compendium of early Manhattan that lasted until the telephone book took over (*The Sense of the Past*); the address book ("Mrs. Medwin"); illustrated books—these are numerous, and also illustrators like Gustave Doré, or the fictional illustrator in "The Real Thing." Best-sellers, that is books as money-making commodities, figure frequently, as do lost manuscripts and incipient books of "blocked" writers which never get beyond talk ("The Coxon Fund"). A prayerbook plays an important role in a brief incident in the

The original version of this essay appeared as "What Henry James's Characters Read and Why: The Books in the Book," in *A. B. Bookman's Weekly,* May 15, 1978, pp. 3468–94.

Jacobs, Pierce & Fuller, drygoods 3 William
Jacobson Jacob L. 309 Broadway h. 200 Bowery
Jacobson Richard S. teacher 200 Elm
Jacobus Augustus L. frames 42 Mott h. 72 Bayard
Jacobus Cornelius C. builder 78 Wooster h. 73 Greene
Jacobus David, framemaker 42 h. 131 Mott
Jacobus David N. sashmaker 138 Wooster h. 71 Laurens
Jacobus Giles, carpenter 60 Avenue 6th c. Barrow
Jacobus James G. lockmaker 217 Church
Jacobus John, lumber 180 Cherry h. 273 Walker
Jacobus Julius, clothier 71 Chatham
Jacobus Lyman A. merchant 66 Cedar h. 55 Bank
Jacobus Thomas, shoemaker 143 Waverley c. Gay
Jacobus Henrietta widow of Nicholas, 74 Carmine
Jacobus & Conklin, builders 78 Wooster
Jacobus D. & A. L. frames 42 Mott
Jacot Edward H. hardware 10 Platt
Jacot Julius, coffeehouse 231 William
Jacot William, hardware 10 Platt
Jacot & Courvoisier, watch-cases 119 Fulton
Jacquelin John M. mer. 6 Southwilliam h. 32 Greenwich
Jacquelin & Allien, 6 Southwilliam
Jacquemond J. B. artificial florist 63 Lispenard
Jacques Francis, merchant 285 Pearl   [vide Jaques
Jacques William, mer. 285 Pearl h. Irving-pl n. Seventeenth
Jacques W. & F. merchants 285 Pearl
Jadownicki Michael B. shirts &c. 67 William
Jaffray & Co Robert, silkgoods 182 Pearl h. 93 Spring
Jaggar John C. bootmaker 52 Gold
Jaggar Walter, broker 55 Wall h. Irving-pl n. Seventeenth
Jaggar John, 49 Cedar h. Brooklyn
Jaggar & Skidmore, drygoods 49 Cedar
Jahne Henry, jeweller 187 Broadway n. Dey h. 50 Crosby
James Alanson, stoves 295 Water
James Daniel, fruits 215 Canal
James Frederic, broker 60 Wall .
James Henry, 21 Washing-place
James Henry A. segarboxes 183 Grand
James John, merchant 18 South h. 10 Wooster
James John W. stove manuf 295 Water
James Morris B. grocer 115 Front c. Wall
James Morris F. forwarder 125 Broad
James Nathaniel E. hardware 92 John
James Perry, 35 Eldridge
James Rachael, 100 Canal
James Richard, bootmaker 231 Broadway h. Gold c. Frankfort
James Thomas, tavern 142 Avenue 8th
James William, 18 South
James William T. foundry 40 h. 35 Eldridge
James William & John, merchants 18 South
James & Co. brokers 60 Wall
Jamieson & Sanford, bakers 154 South
Jamison John, kitchen furn. 255 Greenwich h. 164 Chambers
Jamison Joseph, saddler 8 Old-slip h. 37 Pearl
Jamison Robert, 255 Greenwich c. Murray

Jamison W. & J. kitchen furniture 255 Greenwich See }
    advertisement in the first part of this book   }
Janes Charles B. forwarder, 23 Coenties-sl h. Howard's hotel
Janes Ebenezer S. grocer 130 Cherry h. 6 Market
Janes r. . Edmund S f sec. 115 Nassau h. 26 Lispenard
Janes Horace, broker 12 Wall
Janes Pascal P. stonecutter 38 Leroy
Janes Samuel, stonecutter 38 Gouverneur
Janes Walter R. agent 72 Cedar h. 81 Barrow
Janeway William W. & George, 18 Cityhall-pl
Janeway George, estate of, 5½9 Pearl
Janin Ariene B. broker 46 Broadway h. 428 Broome
Jansen Benjamin G. bookselle 158 Nassau h. Brooklyn
Jansen William H. attorney 33 John c. Nassau
Jansen & Bell, blank stationers 138 ; 158 Nassau
Janssen Herman, grocer 110 William c. John
Janvier Francis D. com mer. 37 South
Janvier & Co. 37 South
Jaques David, 230 Canal
Jaques Edward I. music 176 Prince
Jaques Isaac, tailor 59 John ½
Jaques Isaac, 545 Greenwich   [vide Jacques
Jaques Isaac S. grocer 174 Front h. New-Jersey
Jaques Robert W. painter 41 Leonard
Jaques Samuel J. porter-h 2 Gouv-lane h. 42 Greenwich
Jaques Stephen H. 64 Vandam
Jaques Thomas, tinsmith 332 Grand
Jaques William A. 320 Bleecker
Jaquith Nathaniel C. dryg 229 Greenwich h. 181 Chambers
Jardine George, organbuilder 83 Anthony h. 133 Mercer
Jardine John, organbuilder 79 Laurens
Jarman William G. fruits 6 Charlton
Jaroshinski Basil, hats 307 Hudson
Jarvis Auron, M.D. 218 Bowery h. 163 Chrystie
Jarvis Benjamin, clerk 303 Hudson
Jarvis Charles, portraitpainter 140 Canal
Jarvis Charles A. broker 45 Bank
Jarvis David Sandford, stables 661 Broadway
Jarvis Elkanah, fisherman 5 Sixth
Jarvis Flewwelling, mason 65 Willett
Jarvis George A. merchant 81 Front h. Brooklyn
Jarvis George W. tailor 13 Bedford
Jarvis Grafton, binder 5 Burton
Jarvis Henry, fruits 536 Broome
Jervis Isaac, 16 Eleventh n Bowery
Jarvis James, boardinghouse 32 Vesey
Jarvis Jannet, comb 635 Broadway
Jarvis Jay, grocer 19 Bowery
Jarvis Jeffrey, shoemaker 108 Chatham h. 63 Bayard
Jarvis John M. accountant 30 Greene
Jarvis Jonathan, joiner 462 Water h. 482 Cherry
Jarvis Nathaniel, 20 Cityhall
Jarvis Nelson, draper & tailor 142 Broadway h. 5 Dey
Jarvis Noah, agent 45 Bank
Jarvis Pierre, lumber West n. Hemersley h. 43 Bedford
29

Figure 2. *Longworth's New York Directory*, 1842–43
Sample page shows Henry James, Sr.'s name and address during the year
Henry James the novelist was born.
(Courtesy New York Historical Society; photograph by Kenneth Chen)

ghost story of "Sir Edmund Orme." Dictionaries appear, an Italian one, which helps one of his heroes read Leopardi (whom James read during his early Roman days), and a Greek lexicon which helps the young Morgan Moreen in "The Pupil" find the Greek equivalent for the phrase "gross impertinence."

There are also erotic books, called "naughty" or "unclean" in Victorian days. In the 1879 edition of *The American,* James removes from an earlier printing the erotic classic he had mentioned, *Les Amours du Chevalier de Faublas* (1789–90), a licentious novel by Jean-Baptiste Louvet de Couvray (1760–97) in favor of the more sophisticated *Les Liaisons dangereuses* by Pierre Choderlos de Laclos (1741–1803) a novel about a seducer and his victims (fig. 3). This substitution had already occurred in Balzac's *Eugénie Grandet* in an exchange between the Abbé Cruchot and Madame de Grassins which probably gave James the idea to use the greater suitability of the more refined book as against its predecessor. In his later fiction James would draw on the less inhibited novels of France and Italy.

The materials of authorship are used by James on occasion. Thus, in two short stories, printers' proofs are involved in the central situation. In "The Author of 'Beltraffio' " the proofs of her husband's new book shock the author's wife so profoundly that she decides to withdraw medical help for their son; she would rather have him die than grow up and read the father's corrupting works. In "The Modern Warning," proofs of a book of that name make the American wife of a British critic of the United States insist that he withdraw the volume from publication. Later, a rereading of the proofs results in her changing her mind.

*   *   *

In James's novels and tales, books are read to other characters; they are given as presents in beautiful bindings; they are used for didactic purposes. And certain of his males carry volumes (presumably in small-format editions) in their pockets. Rowland Mallet in *Roderick Hudson* pockets his Wordsworth; the hero in "The Ghostly Rental," an early tale, has Pascal's *Pensées* as a pocket-companion; in "Owen Wingrave," a volume of Goethe's poems in the young would-be soldier's pocket expresses the contrast between Owen's poetic sensibility and the military destiny prescribed for him by his family.

A book in the pocket of Louis Leverett in "The Point of View" is a contemporary example of the great Dutch printers who continued in the nineteenth century to produce fine small books. It is "exquisitely printed, a modern Elzevir," referred to once more as "the little French Elzevir that I love so well." In "Covering End," sixteen years later, another rare book from the other great continental press appears in a metaphor, "She turned it over as if pricing a Greek Aldus." In *The Wings of the Dove,* a book, a Tauchnitz edition (Tauchnitz books appear crucially four times in James's work), is left on an alp, to reverse the usual equation

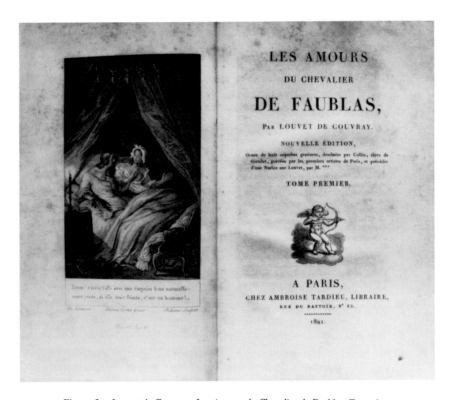

Figure 3.   Louvet de Couvray, *Les Amours du Chevalier de Faublas,* Tome 1
(Paris: Tardieu, 1821)
(Collection Adeline R. Tintner; photograph by Kenneth Chen)

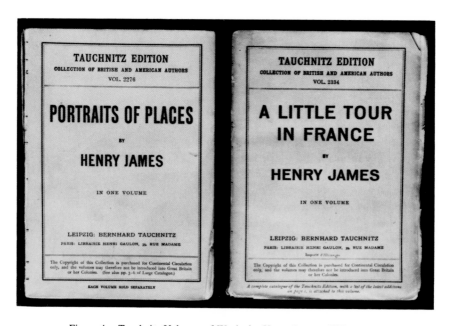

Figure 4.   Tauchnitz Volumes of Works by Henry James, 1880s
Portraits of Places and *A Little Tour in France*
(Collection Adeline R. Tintner; photograph by Kenneth Chen)

that the alp leaves *its* mark in books as in Byron (fig. 4). (In a tale, "The Abasement of the Northmores," a book is printed in a single copy and ordered destroyed after the owner's death.)

Books are presented not only as something to read but in their form as commodities. Herbert Dodd in "The Bench of Desolation" is a bookseller; he delivers books by Lamb and Crabbe (the choice of these two authors is important because Dodd and Kate Cookham are from the social class that these authors write about) (fig. 5). There is a book agency for which Abel Taker ("Fordham Castle") worked. There is also a story devoted to a *preface* to a book ("The Velvet Glove") written after James's series of prefaces to various books, including his own *New York Edition*. Almost as many books are put down unread, as books read. There are also interrupted readings. Books indeed do furnish James's world.

It is my purpose in this essay to select examples of Henry James's use of books in many variant forms to illustrate for readers how much reading "fun" they can obtain by watching closely James's book usage in his fictions. My examples are chosen where they seem illustrative and typical; many more are possible.[1] In James's novels and tales it can be said that there is never an accidental allusion to or quotation from a book. Each reference has its distinct function. Books are the "gauge" by which the novelist and his characters "measure" their minds, as he has Ferdinand, the ailing Civil War veteran, reflect in "A Most Extraordinary Case." There are so many crucial moments derived from the parts books play, that this essay must limit its attention to such books as appear actively in the plot and function significantly, and where the volumes are quoted from, or alluded to, in unmistakably recognizable form; not least where they serve as analogy and underline an issue of the story. I propose to show how, with the passing years, James's book allusions—especially as analogue, and in their subtlety—provide new avenues for critical consideration, source-studies, and contextual readings, now that we have available a listing of the greater part of his library, accumulated during his many years of authorship on both sides of the Atlantic and in his well-travelled European cities. There is also a special category to consider—the book titles James invented within his particular corpus of "tales of the literary life," some of his wittiest and most satirical—and bitterly ironical—stories.

*   *   *

Let us look first at the way James employed established literary works familiar for the most part to all readers. Their prevalence in his fiction shows how the author expects his reader to keep up with him in his literary cultivation. As a young author James expected perhaps too much from his reader and after writing a story like "A Most Extraordinary Case" in 1868, which appears to be a borrowing from *La Chartreuse de Parme* (the nephew loved by an aunt, etc.), there

Figure 5.   *Life and Poems of the Rev. George Crabbe*, 8 Volumes (London:
John Murray, 1854)
Henry James's signature is on the front flyleaf of volume 1.
(Collection Adeline R. Tintner; photograph by Kenneth Chen)

is no mention of Stendhal or his book title. He is learning that the "secret" of his reader's "getting" the literary parallel requires hints and clues. From then on for a while he throws in author or title or both. We see this when James has Miss Condit invoke characters from *The Marble Faun* as analogues to show how "Impressions of a Cousin" draws on the Hawthorne classic. We see it also in thickstrewn form in "Travelling Companions" where Goethe plus George Sand (*La Dernière Aldini*) and Stendhal join with many pictorial masterpieces to create an educative analogue of romanticism by which the young lovers learn their love for one another.

After years of employing such devices James finally arrived at a supremely sophisticated example in *The Ambassadors,* where the reader is expected to pick up more elusive but clearly indicated clues to the interrelation between literary masterpieces and the psychology and action of the novel. By this time we are trained to see, as Jamesian readers, that Strether's mention of his purchase of seventy volumes of Victor Hugo's works is relevant (if obvious) when he enters Notre Dame Cathedral and meets Mme. de Vionnet (*vide* Hugo's *Notre Dame de Paris*). When Strether met Miss Gostrey, in Chester, she recognized his first given names (Lewis Lambert) as the title of a "bad" novel by Balzac. The reader is reminded that in a travel essay James deplored the fact that Balzac never described Chester; Miss Gostrey in turn deplores the fact Balzac never did Woollett, Massachusetts. The reference establishes many connections for the reader, the chief one being the preparation for James's "typical tale of Paris," his tribute to French literature and art. Balzac strikes an opening note as the most representative genius of Paris.[2]

Most of the books read by the characters are classics. Vanderbank and Mrs. Brookenham discuss a character's resemblance to Anna Karenina in *The Awkward Age.* Although Madame de Mauves's inflexible mind has been fed by romantic novels, other women read serious books: Pandora on shipboard reads Sainte Beuve, Alfred de Musset, and Renan. James reviewed Renan's *Souvenirs d'enfance et de jeunesse* for *The Atlantic Monthly* in August 1883, and it is tempting to conjecture that it was this volume that Pandora was reading on shipboard (fig. 6). Her story appeared in June, 1884 in *The New York Sun.* Mrs. Vivian (*Confidence*) reads Victor Cousin; Mary Garland (*Roderick Hudson*) reads Sismondi's *Italian Republics* and Roscoe's *Leo the Tenth.* In fact, the quantity of history consumed by earnest young women in James is extraordinary. In the later novels, such a taste is part of James's strategy. In *The Wings of the Dove,* the heroine and her companion have read Pater, Marbot, Maeterlinck, and Gregorovius, the inclusion of two of these writers showing a special taste for Byzantinism, with emphasis on Gibbon, characteristic of *fin de siècle* personalities. A girl, when dining alone in "The Given Case," props up Gardiner's *History of the Civil Wars* as a kind of Jamesian joke, and also as an allusion to the civil war between men and women—when it is a question of how far flirting is permissible in women as well as in men.

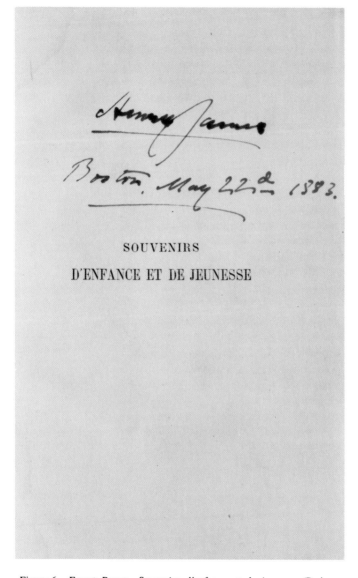

Figure 6. Ernest Renan, *Souvenirs d'enfance et de jeunesse* (Paris:
Calmann Lévy, 1883)
This book was signed: ''Henry James, Boston, May 22d 1883.''
(Collection Adeline R. Tintner; photograph by Kenneth Chen)

In the tale "At Isella," worldly monks talk of Alexander Dumas's *Monte Cristo* and the heroine reminds the narrator of a Stendhal heroine. In "Master Eustace" there is in an upstairs room a volume of the poems of Evariste-Désiré de Parny (1753–1814), a little-known French writer noted for his elegant verse, with the hero's father's signature and date written on the fly-leaf. James had some of his father's books in his library. In an early tale, "Professor Fargo," James uses a classic because of its illustrations. He finds a "tattered volume of *Don Quixote*" and "communed deliciously with the ingenious Hidalgo." He meets a fanatical colonel and recognizes him as Don Quixote in the flesh, "his high browed gentlemanly visage, his wrinkles, his moustache and his sadness." Gustave Doré's famous illustrations of Cervantes were published in 1863 and, as we know, were closely examined by James. The description in the James tale fits the Doré Don, the archetypal image. The literary classic as analogue is continued when James uses Milton's twin poems, "L'Allegro" and "Il Penseroso," to show the tug-of-war between the scholarly life and the worldly life in his hero "Benvolio." The story carries out the analogy (hinted at in the mention of "Il Penseroso") through other details that show he had Milton's poems in hand.

Young girls with books began early to populate James's fiction. In "The Sweetheart of M. Briseux" we have an interpretation of Shelley's "Ode on Dejection near Naples," used to spark the basic incompatibility between the engaged couple, who sometimes read without our knowing what they read, and sometimes with our knowledge. The great instance of this is Isabel Archer in *The Portrait of a Lady,* who is reading an unnamed book when Mrs. Touchett finds her in Albany and takes her to England. From then on Isabel opens books and closes them, but titles are usually blurred (when the situation becomes blurred) after Isabel marries Osmond. Gilbert Osmond opens and closes a book while he is thinking about his wish to marry his daughter off to Lord Warburton. There is, however, one named book by Ampère, given to Isabel by her cousin Ralph, which seems to be an analogue—only in reverse. Jean-Jacques Ampère (1800–1864) was the lover of Madame Récamier and wooed her just as Osmond woos Isabel. Ampère, unlike Osmond, was not a fraud. James had just written in 1875 an article, "The Two Ampères," in which he related that this Ampère had written an *Histoire Romaine* (1858) and, like Osmond, the author of "Rome Revisited," wrote "indifferent rhyme."

Another book reference in *The Portrait* is loaded with meaning. "Osmond was seated at a table near the window with a folio volume before him, propped against a pile of books and Isabel saw that he had been copying from it the drawing of an antique coin." The analogue shows a man of taste who has married her for her money. When Isabel is about to go to the dying Ralph who arranged for her to inherit a fortune, the Countess Gemini "had an open volume in her hand . . . she appeared to have been glancing down a page which failed to strike her as interesting. . . . " She says to Isabel, " 'You, who are so literary, do tell me some amusing book to read! Everything here is so fearfully edifying. Do you think this would do me any good?' Isabel glanced at the title of the volume she held out, but without reading or understanding it.'' One might say that the later book references in *The Portrait* show that even books can give Isabel no pleasure, since she cannot lose herself in literature after her marriage, which is a great loss to her and means she will find no consolation in the real world. In *The Bostonians,* aside from Verena and Olive reading German (Goethe) and history together, Basil Ransom is the only one who reads well-known authors: de Toqueville (since he is interested in the American character and politics) and Thomas Carlyle.

*   *   *

The Princess Casamassima might be called James's "library" book. In it books are exhibited in their various functions and forms. Through reading, Hyacinth gains an education, pulls himself up the social ladder, and makes himself a kind of gentleman. By careful "name-dropping" of books (though not a boring catalogue as in Flaubert's *L'Education sentimentale* on which James may be "improving") we learn that at fifteen he reads Bacon and the social historians, Michelet and Carlyle. When at Medley he is reminded of Keats's "Ode to a Nightingale.'' He recognizes novels by Bulwer in Captain Sholto's flat; he shows Christina that he knows Schopenhauer, which she does, also; he recognizes a character in a Feuillet novel in the princess herself as he reads an installment of it in the *Revue des Deux Mondes*;[3] he discusses Ruskinian theories; he reads Leopardi in Venice and wishes he could lay his hands on some of the writers within "the intensely modern school of advanced and consistent realists" (Zola and the naturalists), which he misses in the somewhat puerile library of Lady Aurora. In contrast to Hyacinth's reading, hers is carefully itemized. "There were several volumes of Lamartine and a set of the spurious memoirs of the Marquise Renée-Caroline de Créqui (d. 1525) which James owned; but for the rest of the little library consisted mainly of Marmontel [Jean-François (1723–99)] and Madame de Genlis [Felicité Ducrest de Saint-Aubin (1746–1830)], *Le Récit d'une soeur* and the tales of M. J. T. de Saint-Germain" (a strange adventurer of the eighteenth century), and although "she did possess a couple of Balzac's novels" by ill luck "they happened to be just those our young man had read more than once." He had felt like a Balzac hero when the princess summoned him at the play. James has selected books to indicate that Hyacinth had the reading background of an educated upper-class man: history, philosophy, the romantic realist novels of Balzac and of Bulwer and a general "acquaintance with the light literature of his country." His reading makes him in the princess's eye "one of the most civilized of little men."

The second role the book plays is the aesthetically satisfying one, the tool to teach Hyacinth beauty. The volume of Lord Bacon had been bound by the best binder in London and leads to a friendship with Poupin, the revolutionary, and so the book becomes the peripety of action, the connecting link between the two conflicting forces, aesthetic and ethical, that tear Hyacinth apart and lead to his suicide. Through the beautiful binding of Bacon's "Essays" the revolutionary idea enters Hyacinth life, and his career as an artisan, a binder of books, is inaugurated.

Its third role is to relate Hyacinth to the women in the novel. He reads Scott and Dickens aloud to Pinnie, his adoptive mother, and later Browning's *Men and Women* to Christina. He also binds a volume of Tennyson with "Russian leather delicately blue tinted" for her, but she isn't there to receive it. The book turned to a virtual "proof and gage," writes James, "as if a ghost had left a palpable relic." Christina, in fact, has found a use for herself in his profession. She hires him as her bookbinder; however, her interest in books fades as her interest in him fades. (She might be said to be an early exponent of "radical chic.") The books cover all kinds of printed matter. Paul Muniment, the young working man, learned from posters and time-tables. In addition to light literature, girl's literature both French and English, and a popular play, there is a curious tea pavilion at Medley where there are *unique* books, "novels that one could not have found any more and were only there," the last of their kind. The true relation lies between the books and Hyacinth, who does not own books but has borrowed them and appropriated their contents. They have, until Millicent and Christina appear, created a life for him, given him his job, introduced him to his romantic conflict.

The Balzacian references in *The Princess* continue a tradition that had begun long before. *The American*'s base in Balzac was acknowledged by James in his 1905 revision, when he has Valentin say, "we're fit for a museum or a Balzac novel." In "A New England Winter" there is a nameless "Balzac novel" which Florimond promises to lend Mrs. Mesh. However, this time there are clues as to which novel it might be. A Watteau fan, the *parent pauvre* (a "poor relative," Rachel Torrance), quotations from Balzac on tea, four definite references in all, suggest Balzac's poor relation novel, *Le Cousin Pons*.[4]

In "The Author of 'Beltraffio,'" Ambient talked "about Balzac and Browning." In *The Tragic Muse* (1890) Gabriel Nash, the taste-maker of his circle, prefers Valerie Marneffe, the high-styled but depraved character in the other *parent pauvre* novel of Balzac, *La Cousine Bette*. The analogue here is of Miriam and her four young men, like Valerie and her four men. Greville Fane, the popular novelist, in another story, had an idea she resembled Balzac, "with Lucien de Rubempré and the Vidame de Pamiers her favorites" although she didn't even know who the latter character was.

*   *   *

The Awkward Age of 1899 is, like *The Princess Casamassima,* a "library" book, planted in a very worldly *fin de siècle* London society—money-oriented, talk-oriented, and dominated by a woman with an informal salon who wants to keep the *status quo* even though her teenage daughter is ready to lead an adult life. Nanda, the daughter, and Aggie, the Anglo-Italian niece of a duchess, have had different upbringings. Aggie, who according to Vanderbank (Van) should be reading Mrs. Radcliffe, reads "stories from English history" anonymously authored, and when she marries Mitch she leaps suddenly to pink novels (French) and even blue ones (Italian). There are unidentified books, rather intriguing and disturbing, like the "large book of facts" that "lay on the young man's [Van's] lap''; Nanda comes out as "Beatrice to his Benedict." The mother fingers "the impossible book, as she pronounced it, that she had taken from him." Nanda, too, "turns over the book." It is all very bookish but nondeterminable. Then there are the other nondetermined books, the "bad" book that Aggie after marriage vulgarly sits on and whose title she keeps from Lord Petherton. This book, although unidentifiable except that it is a French novel, causes a lot of commotion and Nanda admits to having read it.

Against this charming, irresponsible attitude to books, both solemn and frivolous, is posed Mr. Longdon's alternate gifts of highly serious books to Nanda to combat the silliness of those around her and to fight the corruption of the group. He sends her "no end of books . . . her room looks like a bookseller's shop and all in the loveliest bindings, the most standard English works." This serves as a counterthrust to the foreign novels the group reads. The plot involves *The Bostonians* in parody form since it occurs to Mrs. Brook that Longdon is "buying" Nanda (as Olive "bought" Verena), but the books are "thrown in" and will have nothing to do with the money he will leave her as the double of her grandmother whom he loved. Keats, Zola, Virgil, and Tolstoy are invoked. Perhaps the most touching and deadly scene is when Van comes to Nanda's little "library" bedroom and in his guilty embarrassment at having rejected her, he chatters, "What a jolly lot of books—have you read them all? . . . Flowers and pictures and—what are the other things people have when they are happy and superior?—books and birds." Then he mentions heroines he is not sure about. Do they come from Scott or Hugo "or have I got my heroines mixed?" The books get all confused in his mind "or am I muddling up my Zola?"[5] Then, embarrassed when the conversation gets more general, he goes back to the books. "I see you go in for sets . . . I see *big* sets. What's this? Volume 23 of 'The British Poets'? . . . But when the deuce do you, you wonderful being, do you find time to read? *I* don't find any—'tis too hideous. One passes, in London, into illiteracy and barbarism." After the business for which Nanda has summoned Van, and later Mitchy, the book talk drops, as it does in *The Princess;* but it has served its purpose and has followed the pattern of Hyacinth's education. Only here the oddball is the young girl growing up and changing the relations and the balance of power for her mother.

What is singular in the terms of identifiable books is the attention paid to volume 23 of the British Poets, devoted to the poetry of Dryden. It may be, as

Leon Edel has suggested, also a tribute to the twenty-three-volume set of Balzac which James reviewed in 1875. The reference to ''The British Poets'' may have included a reference to other sets such as *The Library of the World's Best Literature,* which came out in thirty volumes from October 1896 to September 1897, published by Peale and Hill in New York. Henry James contributed to volume 12 of this series an essay on Nathaniel Hawthorne, to volume 16 an essay on James Russell Lowell, and to volume 25 an essay on Ivan Turgenev. All three essays were later reprinted, one of them, Hawthorne, in another large set, *The Warner Classics* (volume 2), in 1899. James also contributed an essay to *The International Library of Famous Literature* whose British editor was Richard Garnett, keeper of printed books at the British Museum. The preface was written immediately after *The Awkward Age* and was titled ''The Future of the Novel'' and in it James criticized British fiction for keeping sex on a childhood level— that is, avoiding the subject, thus continuing the theme of *The Awkward Age.* So while Mr. Longdon presents large sets to Nanda Brookenham, the author was deeply involved in writing for big sets of books.

In this way the library enters *The Awkward Age,* seemingly a worldly society novel that would normally have little to do with books. But it is very different from the days of Hyacinth Robinson in 1886. The ''naughty'' book tempts young girls, and it is freely allowed in Mrs. Brook's group but not for the continentally-reared Aggie who may cut loose only after she is married. Nanda has been given such a book by Vanderbank; and Aggie devours them after having been deprived of them in her virginal state. The beautiful bindings are back again, and Longdon's choices are a kind of desperate attempt to fight the dissolution of standards for the teaching of the young. Lady Langrish's girlish and harmless library has disappeared. The book has suddenly gotten wings and, now a kind of ball in a game, while Aggie is chased by Petherton, and she performs her little act of sitting on the book to prevent his finding out which one she has. This bit of drama is the most active scene in which the fight over a book determines the changed relation of the young to the adult and mature members of the group. Where Bacon's *Essays* was the center of *The Princess,* this nameless French novel is at the heart of *The Awkward Age.*

*   *   *

In James's tales of the 1890's we enter, understandably, another kind of book world—a world of James-invented books. These figure in his remarkable and comparatively neglected ''tales of the literary life'' written alongside his ghostly tales of this period. The invented books are often simply satirical titles: they make fun of popular writers who are a success, as against troubled artists who are failures. Some of the writers have undergone gender changes. Males masquerade under female pen-names. Females take on male nomenclature (fig. 7). These

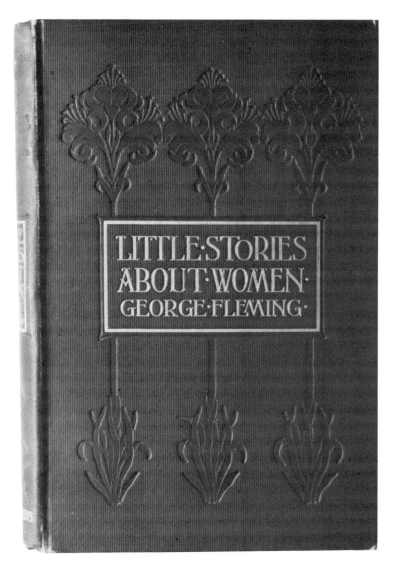

Figure 7. George Fleming (Constance Fletcher), *Little Stories about Women* (London: Grant Richards, 1897)
Henry James's signature is on the half-title page.
(Collection Adeline R. Tintner; photograph by Kenneth Chen)

stories also mock the literary marketplace and the public taste, the best-seller world. "The Middle Years," written when James reached fifty, is an invented title which gives its name to the James story about a book and its writer. Its author is a "fingerer" of style, a reviser of his texts, and the story vividly voices James's quest for perfection. (Three other tales have the titles of invented books—"The Modern Warning," "The Author of 'Beltraffio,' " and "Nona Vincent," which is the name of an unpublished but performed play. In "The Private Life" a play is written while the story is told, but is finished after the story ends.)

In "The Death of the Lion," Neil Paraday, a neglected writer, is discovered by a journalist and quite suddenly becomes a literary lion. No one reads him, but he is taken up by society. At a country house he shares billing with two other writers with switched genders. Guy Walsingham turns out to be a woman and her book is called "Obsessions." Dora Forbes turns out to be a whiskered male whose book has a tongue-in-cheek title "The Other Way Round." Paraday dies of his fame, after his valuable final manuscript is lost as it passes from hand to hand among his nonreading admirers. Actual books invoked in this story are by Flaubert, Hannah More, and Schiller to add a touch of reality beside James's satirical inventions.

In "The Next Time," Ray Limbert, a delicate and dedicated fictional artist, tries again and again to ""make a silk purse into a sow's ear"" in order to have a novel that will sell; but each time he can only produce a greater nonselling master-piece. He marries on "The Major Key" and writes "The Hidden Heart" but dies in the midst of a fragmentary novel called "Derogation"—still a failure in his obsessive attempt to injure his own reputation. The hunt for the "secret" in Hugh Vereker's style or content in all his fiction, in James's famous "The Figure in the Carpet," lists no invented novels by Vereker, but Gwendolyn, one of the hunters, manages to produce two mediocre works on which James bestows the titles "Deep Down" and "Overmastered," as all the hunters have been.

An important invented book is to be found in James's unfinished novel, *The Sense of the Past*. This represents, in codified form, a notion of history that is subsumed in Ralph Pendrel's desire to visit a past still visitable in his inherited house in England. The notion of history appears early in the novel where Aurora Coyne, the monied heiress, quotes from Ralph's "Essay in Aid of the Reading of History." It is this essay which won him the English inheritance; the dream of the past is initiated by the book. (He earned it by his "pen" which is con-trasted, in his name, to the "coin" in Aurora's name.) The novel is an ultimate rewriting of James's early tale, "A Passionate Pilgrim," where Clement Searle failed to have his dream of owning an English manor house come true. The similarity between the Reynolds portrait of Pendrel's ancestor and himself acts in *The Sense of the Past* as the agent of transposition into the year 1820—a year probably chosen by James for his own "visitable past," the time when his grand-father, William James of Albany, was still alive as were his various "windows in the past''—certain friendly old ladies in London James admired—Mrs. Kemble, Mrs. Procter, and Mrs. Duncan Stewart.

Other invented books are found in the early ''Benvolio'' (1875) but they are without titles. Mark Ambient in ''The Author of 'Beltraffio' ''—as the title tells us—is James's first author to have a named book. There are books in ''The Aspern Papers,'' again unnamed, Jeffrey Aspern having been a sort of Shelley or Byron of early American literature in James's private fictional literary world. The ''master'' in ''The Lesson of the Master'' has written a book called ''Shadowmere'' and the novice has made his debut with ''Ginistrella.'' The last of the imagined novels is to be found in the story called ''The Velvet Glove'' (1908) at a time when James's New York Edition had taken much of his time. The hero has written a ''slightly too fat'' novel, *The Heart of Gold,* which has been dramatized (probably a nostalgic glance backward at *The Golden Bowl*). A beautiful princess, who has written a novel called ''The Top of the Tree,'' tries to woo Berridge into writing a preface for her new novel ''The Velvet Glove'' (a pun on her strategy since her glove conceals an iron fist). Berridge declines and bestows a kiss instead. Here James's varied list of invented novels ends on a note of high romance and in a mock-epical format.

*   *   *

Pointing in the direction of James's ghostly tales, most of them written in the 1890s, are allusions to Sheridan Le Fanu (1814–73), the Irish master of the supernatural, and Wilkie Collins (1824–89), the English creator of detective fiction. Le Fanu is mentioned in ''The Liar'' (1888) where the portrait painter is so fascinated by one of his stories that he is late for dinner. In this tale, James infers that lying in art is valid, but telling lies in life is corrupting. If Colonel Capadose, in the story, had made more art out of his fantasies, he would have been justified; Le Fanu invented tales that could not have happened, but his fictional fantasies were artistic and so he had validity. In ''Maud-Evelyn'' (1900) James has a lady interrupted in her reading of ''a successful novel of the day'' by the son of an old friend, Marmaduke. She allows that he supersedes Wilkie Collins, so that she never finishes the Wilkie Collins novel. James, however, finishes it in his own way, for he seems to be redoing Collins's *The Woman in White*—the dead wife and the living wife and the inheritance finally bestowed on the live (would-be) wife, after the others die. In the Collins novel, the drawing master inherits the house and its valuable contents, as the hero of James's story does.

In James's masterpiece of the supernatural, ''The Turn of the Screw,'' only one book is mentioned, although others are alluded to indirectly. The governess remembers ''that the book I had in my hand was Fielding's *Amelia*.'' She is ''deeply interested in my author'' but is distracted by the ghost of Peter Quint. Why she has been given *Amelia* to read may be related to the fact that Edmund

Gosse, James's close friend, had published during the same year as "The Turn of the Screw" a new edition of Fielding's works. James wrote to Gosse, September 14, 1898, that he took a trip to the country near Tenterden, "The really grand old bravely British village—transporting almost to your Fielding moment and medium." Then he comments on the preface to the edition and says that Gosse should have neglected "all biographical facts" and devoted his limited space to "a picture of the nature of the man's imagination and of the world—the image of life—that ressort from his volumes."[6]

James's "The Turn of the Screw" came out a few weeks after this letter. It seems probable that Gosse and he had been discussing Fielding and that James had a very definite opinion and clearcut impression of Fielding's talents. The bringing in of *Amelia* is, in a way, a kind of tribute to his friend's labors. Why *Amelia* and not *Tom Jones?* What novel of Fielding's would the governess be reading except *Amelia,* a sentimental heroine, a young woman who suffers because she loves Captain Booth (very like the remote master in Harley Street or even Quint)? Amelia is in a state of hysteria analogous to that of James's governess. Fielding's governess suffers from direct pressures—the tendency of the gentry to seduce girls of the lower class: her efforts are centered on avoiding this sexual pressure and protecting her two children, a boy and a girl, of similar age to Miles and Flora, from the corruptions of the gift-offering seducers. The governess in James's story is not as exposed as Amelia: her pressures are psychological, they come from within—and from her anxieties on finding herself in an unfamiliar world.

* * *

A striking feature in James's novels is the way in which characters open books, or read books, with little attention to what is on the page: it seems a kind of action that was later superseded in modern novels by characters lighting and extinguishing cigarettes. Thus in the early story "A Light Man," James describes a wealthy elderly Mr. Sloane whose two passions are reading and talking; yet even as stimulus to conversation, he always has a book in his hand: the number of un-named and unspecified books in this story is almost uncountable. Mentioned at least twice in *Roderick Hudson* are "books of facts" that Christina Light asks Rowland Mallet to recommend, for she says she is "tired of novels."

Isabel Archer, in *The Portrait of a Lady,* seems in a constant fidget with books to help her out—books whose titles we cannot even guess. In her childhood in Albany (like Henry James as a boy in the same city) she had "uncontrolled use of a library full of books with frontispieces." In "At Isella" the young hero recognizes "the steel plates of my infancy . . . the old steel plates in a French book that I used to look at as a child." In England, Isabel is always opening books and shutting them. Married to Osmond in Italy, she seems equally restless and in the same way. Sometimes she is so disturbed she cannot make out the words on the page.

Sometimes James uses color, especially in his allusions to continental paper-bound books, to identify volumes in a general way. Thus in "The Story in It" we have lemon- and blue-covered French and Italian books, with the author of only one book named, Gabriele D'Annunzio, to set the tone of the handling of a love affair and how it can be defined. The books are also characterized as to content, when not individually identified. What they are about, and how they affect the characters, is clearly expressed in the conversation they stimulate. Occasionally James alludes to the color of English books, as in "Greville Fane," where the narrator sees Miss Fane's "three new volumes, in green, in crimson, in blue, on the book table that groaned with light literature" at his club, a characteristic Jamesian oxymoron.

*   *   *

With all this play of color and allusion for the unidentified books, we come upon some that are never named but sound as if they were written by James himself. There are usually sufficient clues in the narrative. This is particularly true of his early stories about the American girl abroad, where he seems to make himself out to be the oracle on this subject. Daisy Miller, Isabel Archer, the young women in "An International Episode," present themselves as parallels and points of measurement; characters with problems in the stories seem to profit by the comparisons. James treats his work as belonging to "world literature." We have, in this, complicated reader-participation problems.

The first story to contain within it a reference to a book that might be *The Portrait of a Lady* is "Lady Barberina" written three years after this novel. Lady Barb, in a way, is also a portrait of a "lady." This time she is a genuine earl's daughter who has married an American doctor and feels she has been imprisoned in New York. In the scene between Isabel and Osmond in *The Portrait,* Isabel has been reading a book; a fireplace figures in it, and she has just had an interview with Warburton. In the parallel scene in "Lady Barberina," Jackson Lemon, Lady Barb's American husband, is trying to get her to be nicer to his friends. His wife is reading a "stiff little book." Her husband asks her whether she doesn't like it in New York, and she answers, " 'I knew you expected me to live here, but I didn't know you expected me to like it.' She got up from her chair and tossed the volume she had been reading into the empty seat . . . 'I recommend you to read that book . . . It's an American novel.' " When he says he never reads novels she answers, "You had better look into that one; it will show you the kind of people you want me to know." A little later her husband, like Osmond, "turned about to the fire . . . " and he says, "You really must be at home on Sundays, you know. . . . You had better begin today." He might be Osmond laying down the law. When he says he is going to his mother's, Lady Barb answers, " 'And you might take her that book.' 'What book?' 'That nasty one I've been reading.' 'Oh, bother your books!' '' The temptation for the reader of James is to hazard a guess that the book in question is *The Portrait of a Lady* (because of the identical trap both young women find themselves in, because of the pun on "lady" in the title, and because of the similar structure of the two scenes where the husband more or less constrains the lady in question to conform to his demands while seated before a fire and equipped with a book). It is doubly tempting to do this since another tale of the same period, "Pandora," actually names "Daisy Miller"—it is being read by the young German diplomat in a Tauchnitz edition and the American young lady in the story has planted herself in front of him as Daisy did. She also has a brother like the candy-eating brother of Daisy and is called "a Daisy Miller *en herbe.*"

Published in 1882, "The Point of View," an epistolary tale, has a clear allusion to Henry James—it can be to no other writer. A French academician, M. Lejaune, claims the Americans "have a novelist with pretensions to literature, who writes about the chase for the husband and the adventures of rich Americans in our old corrupt Europe, where their primeval candour puts the Europeans to shame." He finds the tale well written but "terribly pale." This suggests "An International Episode."

*   *   *

The fullest and most highly developed example in James's work of this insinuation of his own books occurs at the end of *The Golden Bowl.* Maggie, the heiress who has married an Italian prince, has finally managed to establish a relationship once more with her husband. His mistress, Maggie's former friend, has been psychologically cut off from him. She has won her difficult battle by the quietest kind of silent manipulation but now her sympathy for her abandoned former friend makes her attempt to try to find a way to give her a face-saving escape from her defeat. A book figures as the essential artifact that replaces the earlier and now broken golden bowl. Charlotte has carried off "the dark cover of a volume," part of "an old novel that the Princess had . . . mentioned having brought down from Portland Place in the charming original form of its three volumes." Charlotte had hailed, with a specific glitter of interest, "the opportunity to read it, and our young woman had . . . directed her maid to carry it to Mrs. Verver's apartments. She was afterwards to observe that this messenger . . . had removed but one of the volumes, which happened not to be the first. Still possessed . . . of the first while Charlotte . . . was helplessly armed with the second, Maggie prepared to sally forth with succour. The right volume . . . was all she required—in addition . . . to the bravery of her idea." She will set things *right* with the *right volume.* Maggie "held up her volume" timidly to show that Charlotte should not fear her and quavered that she couldn't bear to think "you should find yourself here without the beginning of your book . . . you've got the wrong volume, and

I've brought you out the right.'' To Charlotte, ''Pride had become the mantle caught up for protection'' and ''she flung it round her as a denial of any loss of her freedom.'' After she ''had uttered thanks for the book . . . which . . . with her second volume she perhaps found less clever than she expected . . . she let Maggie approach sufficiently closer to lay . . . the tribute in question on the bench and take up obligingly its superfluous mate.'' She then speaks as if she is creating her own freedom and tells Maggie that she is ''tired'' of the life she has been leading and that she ''dreams another dream to take Adam [Maggie's father and Charlotte's husband] home—to his real position.'' Charlotte also says that Maggie has worked against her to keep her father for herself. Maggie pretends she has, and has failed. Thus Charlotte's pride is assuaged: '' 'Now I see that you loathed our marriage.' Charlotte had . . . possessed herself mechanically of one of the volumes of the relegated novel and then, more consciously, flung it down again: she was in presence, visibly of her last word. She opened her sunshade . . . she twirled it on her shoulder.'' As she walks away she queries in her pride, ''You haven't worked against me?'' Maggie answers, '' 'What does it matter—if I've failed?' 'You recognize then that you've failed?' . . . Maggie waited; she looked, as her companion had done a moment before, at the two books on the seat. She put them together, and laid them down; then she made up her mind. 'I've failed!' she sounded out before Charlotte, having given her time, walked away. She watched her, splendid and erect, float down the long vista; then she sank upon a seat. Yes, she had done all.''

This most crucial scene in a very long book is enacted between the two women who, with the aid of a book—the right volume—resolve their deepest struggle with each other over the possession of the prince. The object which offers itself as a strategem, so that Maggie may demonstrate the furthest reaches of both her intelligence and her compassion is an old-fashioned three-decker novel (let us say 1881, a generation old would make it ''old''). It is a novel which is fairly ''important,'' since Charlotte looked for the opportunity to read it. The maid, however, had made the mistake in taking her the second volume which Charlotte could not have read, although she pretended to, since she would have seen it was not the beginning. When Maggie says, ''You've got the wrong volume. I've brought you out the right,'' the reader senses more is meant than what is said. The *double entendre* is clear. We are treated to a greater emphasis in the placing of the book than seems necessary. Maggie puts down the book, we are told, and takes up the first volume. The reader begins to feel there is portentousness in the careful recording of the placing of the two volumes of the unidentified old novel. When Maggie feeds Charlotte the lines to make her feel she has not suffered humiliation, Charlotte, in her perturbation, picked up ''mechanically one of the volumes of the relegated novel, and then more consciously flung it down again.'' Now the books are in disorder on the bench. Just before Maggie delivers the final remark that clinches for Charlotte the feeling that she herself has won out in their struggle, "she looked, as her companion had done a moment before, at the two books on the seat; she put them together and laid them down; then she made up her mind. 'I've failed,' she sounded out." Charlotte had thrown the books, or rather flung them down; Maggie had put them in order. She "had done all." This is necessary, for James is implying that Maggie, through her intelligent manipulation of the situation has, so to speak, written the third volume of this so far nameless book!

I think that James wanted the reader to see this book as a definite book, as one of his own and the only one which would fit the physical description he has given us and which would be giving us another form of the same kind of situation the two women find themselves in. It is my opinion that James considered he was doing *The Portrait of a Lady* over again and improving on its original unresolved ending. The dark cover could describe the first dark blue edition of *The Portrait of a Lady* (1881), in its three-volume form. It had never been reprinted after its second three-decker revised version in 1883, as part of James's first collected edition. Charlotte would be interested in reading it at this time in her own predicament, because Maggie had read it, had recommended it, and probably told her it was about an American woman trapped in a marriage from which she chooses *not* to secede, a woman married to a man who collected beautiful things (like Adam Verver). When Maggie offers her the right volume, and says Charlotte has the wrong volume, *this* is the right one, she seems to be saying; "I am offering you the correct way not only to read this book, but to rewrite it. Don't begin with the second volume; read it in correct order." One notices that the third volume is not ever involved in this interaction between the two books and the two women. There seems to be a point to its omission, and the clue is given by the fact that after Charlotte has messed up the books, Maggie puts them in their proper order. She regulates them, as she is regulating her personal drama. She lays the two books together as if she, we are led to speculate, is writing her own version of the third. In *The Portrait of a Lady* Isabel remains immured in her prison. Maggie's rewriting of it, through her own action (to which Charlotte responds) frees both women from the deterministic outcome of *The Portrait of a Lady,* the plot of which readers to this day find left "up in the air."

Maggie has put down the books "on the seat." She sits down, perhaps next to them. "I have done all," she says to herself. She has become the third volume next to the other two. If Charlotte is Isabel revived, then she is now made free by Maggie's power, or at least she can act as if she is free. As if she were a *bozzetto* or small model of James himself, so artfully engaged in rewriting the books of others, Maggie puts herself on record as rewriting by herself a book by her creator. And in this the creator gets a final chance to rewrite it himself. The book-work has been done, and the reader has to join in the game with Maggie. We, too, must do all, must make all the connections. In imposing on the reader the need to respond to his responsibility as an active participant in the book itself,

James forces him to join in the rewriting of the book through his creative *reading* of the book. The reader and the writer thus become ultimately one through their involvement with the characters in *their* book drama.

*   *   *

We may return to *The Princess Casamassima* (1886), Henry James's "library book," to learn how deeply he was interested in fine printing and the binding of books. He does not parade a catalogue of such things, but when the occasion comes for him to specify a certain kind of book, he mentions the work of a real printer or he specifies the conditions under which it is bound in terms of its actual circumstances in the London of the 1880s.

In the novel James tries to show how young Hyacinth Robinson, deprived of a formal education, could still develop his rare sensibility through exposure to fine books, well printed, beautifully bound, and sensibly chosen from the world's great literature. From an early age he is directed in this by his mentor, Anastasius Vetch, who gives him, as we have already noted, a copy of Bacon's *Essays* to start him off. It is "a little cloth-bound volume, a Pickering" which he takes to be bound by "the prince of binders," a Mr. Crickenden, where "the most brilliant craftsman in the establishment," Eustache Poupin, handles the job. It is interesting that the Keynes bibliography of Pickering[7] lists an 1836 edition, clothbound, of Bacon's *Essays,* so we see that James, ever a realist, is describing an existing book.[8] (A copy of this book is in the New York Public Library; see fig. 8.)

It is equally interesting, and indicative of his knowledge of bookbinding standards, that the binder in *The Princess* is a Frenchman, since it shows that James was aware that of the two greatest bookbinders in London at the time one was a Frenchman, Robert Rivière (1808–82). Bacon, "the great Elizabethan," is then bound by the French bookbinder in the story with "a new coat—a coat of full morocco, discreetly, delicately gilt." The binder, M. Poupin, then invites Mr. Vetch to "see his small collection in morocco, Russia, parchment" purely for the love of the thing itself.

Hyacinth thus is initiated into the beauties of fine bookbinding. M. Poupin "showed him his bindings, the most precious trophies of his skill, and it seemed to Hyacinth on the spot he was initiated into a fascinating mystery." In this way the Pickering Bacon bound by the great French binder introduces Hyacinth to his career of bookbinding, for "a charming handicraft was a finer thing than a 'vulgar' business." On the other hand, it also exposes him to the influence of the revolutionary underground with which Poupin is closely involved.

This dichotomy was part and parcel of the craftsman's social dilemma that was solved in England by William Morris's circle with its native socialism. Brought to the extremes of conspiratorial revolution by continental agitators such

THE ESSAYS

OR COUNSELS CIVIL AND MORAL

AND WISDOM OF THE ANCIENTS

OF FRANCIS LORD VERULAM

EDITED BY B. MONTAGU ESQ.

LONDON

WILLIAM PICKERING

1836

Figure 8.   Title Page of Francis Bacon's *The Essays, or Counsels Civil and Moral, and Wisdom of the Ancients* of Francis, Lord Verulam, edited by B. Montagu, Esq. (London: W. Pickering, 1836)
(Courtesy The New York Public Library)

as the Poupin circle in *The Princess,* it creates the dilemma which Hyacinth tragically resolves. The conflict between the aesthetic elements of its artisan activity and its social imperatives prove too much for a young man who was himself a poet *manqué.*[9]

Hyacinth's bookbinding expertise is manifested by his criticism of the poor editions in the other personal libraries introduced into the book, which examines many of the aspects of the role the book plays in human life. The puerile library of the aristocratic do-gooder, Lady Aurora, and the inferior bindings of Captain Sholto whose vulgarity of taste is thereby displayed even though he is a gentleman, do not rate highly in the young master-binder's superior book judgment, but he is also aware of the collector's appeal in the "row of novels out of date and out of print that one couldn't have found anymore and were only there" in one of the pavilions on the country estate at Medley. There, too, in the library of the great house, Hyacinth "came upon rare bindings and extracted previous hints."

His skill also acts as the pretext for the princess to hire him as her personal bookbinder while her interest in him is still intense. He tells her that "cobbled" leather is bad for bookbinding and that in his opinion a woman, "even the most cultivated is incapable of feeling the difference between a bad book and a good," thus endowing his art with a mystique for the great lady. However, she soon finds that "the delight of dainty covers" was no longer fitting as a pastime in a society going up "in flames."

"The little bastard book-binder" now becomes "a master hand" at his profession and one can be sure that when he took up a copy of Tennyson's poems and "devoted himself to the task of binding the book as perfectly as he knew how" the covered book was a masterpiece of binding. The two beautiful books, the Pickering Bacon that started him on his career and the Tennyson custom-bound volumes of poetry that symbolically bind to him the most "remarkable woman in Europe," act as concrete attestations of the practical intelligence and the poetic genius of the country and the man, of England and of Hyacinth who "sprang up" for James "out of the London pavement."

In the collection of James's books at Lamb House there is at least one fine example of great printing and some bindings by the greatest binders of the mid-nineteenth century. A Baskerville three-volume edition of *The Works of William Congreve,* 1761, bound in old calf gilt with yellow edges, is an acknowledged masterpiece of the great printer. James's library at his death also contained two bindings by Francis Bedford. We are told by Brander Matthews in *Old and New Bookbindings* that Quaritch "in his catalogue of bookbinding speaks of Francis Bedford as the best binder who ever lived."[10] The first of James's books was *The Dramatic Works* of John Ford in two volumes, with notes by W. Gifford, library edition, calf extra, gilt and marbled edges, 1827. The second Bedford binding in his library was a two-volume first edition of Robert Browning's *Men and Women,* 1855, yellow calf extra, gilt-edged. It is most significant that after the princess, identifying herself with ''the people,'' moves to a lower-class neighborhood, Hyacinth visits her and brings with him to read to her Browning's *Men and Women*. James's own feelings for the aptness here of an analogue in the great poems by Browning with the situation in which Hyacinth finds himself vis-à-vis the princess, makes him put one of the great books in his own library in the hands of his hero.

The fact that Poupin, the skilled French bookbinder in the novel, was modeled on Rivière, the great bookbinder actually functioning in London during the 1880s, is further emphasized by the appearance in James's library at Lamb House of a set of five volumes of *The Works of Plato,* translated by Benjamin Jowett, 1892, Oxford Press, polished calf extra, top-edged with gilt and bound by Rivière. The publication date indicates that the books had to have been purchased by James after he had published *The Princess* in 1886, so that we may assume that James's interest in Rivière was more than accidental and that he bought the books because he himself had through his own art created in himself a demand for fine bindings by a master-binder of his own time whom he had fictionalized in his novel. James had close friends in the literary world in London who had special interests in books and who were authors of books on books, like Edmund Gosse and, in particular, Andrew Lang, whose books on that subject are singularly plentiful. Lang's *The Library* (London, Macmillan, 1881) preceded *The Princess* by five years and an uncut presentation copy of the book can be found in the Lamb House library. The chances are that James read it either in the Athenaeum or in the Reform Club libraries, or, what is more likely, discussed the book and books with Lang over lunch, since he was meeting him and Gosse daily at the Reform Club during the early 1880s just prior to his writing *The Princess.*

We have seen how in James's *The Awkward Age* (1899), Mr. Longdon fights the corruption of taste in literature and morals of Mrs. Brook's circle by bombarding Nanda with books—classics, ''sets'' and beautifully bound volumes as opposed to the lemon-colored French novels of adultery that the young people are carelessly exposed to by their elders. Nanda has arranged these gifts in her own library ''with an eye to the effect of backs'' and a visitor is struck by the books' appearance. ''Where did you learn so much about bindings?'' Nanda is asked. Her books are ''the most standard English works'' and ''all, in the loveliest bindings.'' James's care for the appearance of his New York Edition, his supervision of ''the plum-coloured'' cloth bindings, his personal concern over the type and size of the margins, all indicate an aesthetic predisposition in regard to the publication of his selected *Novels and Tales.*

From the memorandum James sent to his publisher, Scribner's, on 30 July 1905, we learn that his ''idea has been to arrange for a handsome 'definitive edition.' '' He mentions to Scribner's that their complete edition of Rudyard Kipling ''offers to my mind the right type of form and appearance, the right print and size of page, for our undertaking'' and that he should be ''quite content to have it taken for model.'' However, he specified he would ''like a cover of another colour to differentiate'' his set.[11] Compared to the Kipling set the James edition appears more subdued and refined. In a letter of 14 September 1906, he asks that ''as pretty type as possible'' be used for his *Prefaces.* When the first two volumes of the New York Edition arrive as a kind of New Year's present from his publishers, he replies on 31 December 1907, that he is ''delighted with the appearance, beauty and dignity of the Book—am in short almost ridiculously proud of it. . . . The whole is a perfect felicity.''[12] The margins, the type, and the frontispieces which he had carefully worked over with his photographer, whom he had carefully chosen, bear witness to the great respect he had for the appearance of his own books. Clearly, his fastidiousness as an artist did not stop at the fashioning of his fiction but extended to the whole book, as an object of art as well as a container of meaningful prose.

The rarest book—in reality a metaphor—in all of James's fiction is actually a young woman, for so Kate Croy appears in the eyes of Merton Densher, her lover: ''The women one meets—what are they but books one has already read? You're a whole library of the unknown, the uncut. . . . Upon my word I've a subscription!'' James liked the figure so much that he repeated a version of it in a later chapter of *The Wings of the Dove:* ''He had compared her once, we know, to a 'new book,' an uncut volume of the highest, rarest quality; and his emotion (to justify that) was again and again like the thrill of turning the page.'' This figure appears in the novel just before Kate consents to visit him in his rooms, and we may make of that what we will.

Notes

1. A fuller account of all the books mentioned in James's fiction may be found in my ''What Henry James's Characters Read and Why: The Books in the Book.'' *A. B. Bookman's Weekly,* May 15, 1978, pp. 3468–94.

2. Adeline R. Tintner, ''Balzac's 'Madame Firmiani' and James's *The Ambassadors,''* *Comparative Literature* 25 no. 2, (Spring 1973): 128–35.

3. Adeline R. Tintner, ''Octave Feuillet, *La Petite Comtesse,* and Henry James,'' *Revue de Littérature Comparée* 48, no. 2 (1974): 218–32.

4. Adeline R. Tintner, ''Henry James and a Watteau Fan,'' *Apollo* (June 1974): 488.

5. For a breakdown of the actual books Van mentions see Jean Frantz Blackall's ''Literary Allusion as Imaginative Event,'' *Modern Fiction Studies* 26 (1980): 179–97.

6. Letter of Henry James to Edmund Gosse, dated Lamb House, 14 September 1898, MS. Duke University.

7. Sir Geoffrey Keynes, *William Pickering, Publisher: A Memoir and a Check List of his Publications* (London, Galaxy Press, 1924), p. 50. ''Bacon, Francis, The Essays and Wisdom of the Ancients, ed. by B. Montague, London, 1836.'' I wish to thank Professor Terry Belanger of Columbia University for information in regard to William Pickering.

8. Francis Bacon, *The Essays or Councils, Civil and Moral,* and *Wisdom of the Ancients* of Francis Bacon, Lord Verulam, edited by B. Montague, Esquire (London: W. Pickering, 1836).

9. Adeline R. Tintner, "Keats and James and *The Princess Casamassima,*" *Nineteenth Century Fiction* 28, no. 2, (September 1973): 179–93.

10. Brander Matthews, *Bookbindings Old and New* (New York: Macmillan, 1895), p, 107.

11. *Henry James Letters,* ed. Leon Edel, 4 (Cambridge: Harvard University Press, 1984), p. 366.

12. *Henry James Letters,* 4: 484.

13. A fuller account of this material appeared in *A. B. Bookman's Weekly* (April 3, 1978), pp. 2406–10, and republished in *A. B. Bookman's Yearbook,* 1978, *Part One: The New & the Old,* pp. 44–46.

Index

This index is designed to include references to both the text of this book and to subjects contained in the books owned by James, found in the library list on pages 19–67 of this volume. References to subjects in the library list are made to the appropriate author.

given to Harvard, 9; books, from Lamb House, 15; clothes, disposal of, 6–7; death of, 6; inventory of Lamb House Library, 8; James's books, disposal of, 2; on T. Bosanquet, 7

James, John, 9

James, Peggy (Mrs. Bruce Porter), 3, 15

James VI. *See library list under Lang*

James, William (brother), 3, 11; attitude toward James's library, 7–8

James, Mrs. William, 7

James, William (grandfather), 84

James, William (son), 15

Jesus. *See library list under Strauss*

Joan of Arc. *See library list under France; Wallon*

John, Duke of Argyll. *See library list under Stuart*

Johnson, Samuel, 5. *See also library list under Boswell; Hill*

Jonson, Ben. *See library list under Swinburne*

Jowett, Benjamin, trans., *The Works of Plato,* Rivière binding, 93–94

Karénine, Mme, biography of George Sand, 4

Keats, John: "Ode to a Nightingale," use in *The Princess Casamassima,* 79; use in *The Awkward Age,* 81

Kemble, Frances Ann, 84. *See also library list under Fitzgerald, E.; Kemble*

Kent (England). *See library list under Cobbett*

Kerouaille, Louise de. *See library list under Forneron*

Keynes, Sir Geoffrey, bibliography of Pickering, 91

Kipling, Rudyard: autograph copies of, 2, 4–6; Scribner's edition of, 95

Laclos, Pierre Choderlos de, *Les Liaisons dangereuses,* use in *The American,* 71

La Fontaine, Jean de. *See library list under Taine*

Lamartine, Alphonse-Marie-Louis de Prat de, use in *The Princess Casamassima,* 79

Lamb, Charles, 74. *See also library list under Lucas*

Lamb House

—bindings, of Jowett's *The Works of Plato,* by Rivière, 93–94

—books in, 3; disposal of, 2, 6; Fabes's storage of, 7, 15–16; Fogel inventory, 16–17; printing, by Bedford, 93

—entry, *frontispiece*

—Garden Room: books in, 3–5; destroyed, 6; James's work in, 4

—given to National Trust, 7

—Green Room, books in, 2–4

—inherited by D. James, 6

—memorial room, 7; books in, 8

—Oak Room, books in, 4

—tenancy, of E. F. Benson, 3

—upstairs Winter Writing Room, *18*

Lamplighter, The, 1

Lang, Andrew, *The Library,* 94

Le Fanu, Sheridan, 85; use in "The Liar," 85

Leonardo da Vinci. *See library list under Clement*

Leopardi, Alessandro: use in *The Princess Casamassima,* 79

Lévy, Arthur, 4

Lewes (England). *See library list under Patmore*

Libraries, James and: Athenaeum, 69; London Library, 5; Redwood Library, 69; Reform Club, 69

Library of the World's Best Literature, James's essays in: on Hawthorne, 82; on Lowell, 82; on Turgenev, 82

Lincoln, Abraham. *See library list under Nicolay and Hay*

Literature, English. *See library list under Brooke; Gosse; Taine*

Literature, French. *See library list under Brunetière*

Lockhart, John Gibson. *See library list under Lang*

London (England). *See library list under Besant; Loftie; Pennant; Stow; Wheatley and Cunningham; Wheatley, H. B.*

London Bridge. *See library list under Thomson*

London Library: Carlyle and, 5; James's membership in, 5

Long Island: James house, books from, 9

Longworth's New York Directory, 70

Lowell, James Russell, James's essay on, 82

"Lucia" books, 3

Lutèce. *See library list under Heine*

Lynne (England). *See library list under Kent-Smith*

Lytton, Edward George Earle (Bulwer-Lytton), use in *The Princess Casamassima,* 79

Macdonald, Marshal, 4. *See also library list under Macdonald*

Maeterlinck, Maurice-Polydore-Marie-Bernard, use in *The Wings of the Dove,* 76

Manet, Edouard, repainting of Raphael in *Le Déjeuner sur l'Herbe,* 11

"Mapp" books, 3

Quaritch, Bernard, on F. Bedford, 93

Rachel, Mlle. *See library list under D'Heylli*
Radcliffe, Mrs. Ann, use in *The Awkward Age,* 80
Raleigh, Sir Walter. *See library list under Gosse*
Raphael. *See library list under Clement*
Récamier, Jeanne-Françoise-Julie-Adélaïde: and Ampère, 78. *See also library list under Constant*
Le Récit d'une soeur, use in *The Princess Casamassima,* 79
Reculver. *See library list under Kent-Smith*
Redwood Library (Newport), 69
Reform Club, 94; library, James's use of, 69
Renan, Ernest, 4, 76, 77; *Souvenirs d'enfance et de jeunesse,* James's review of, 76, 77. *See also library list under Darmesteter*
Revue des Deux Mondes, 79
Richborough. *See library list under Kent-Smith*
Richelieu, Cardinal. *See library list under Michelet*
Rivière, Robert, 91; bindings by, 13; bindings, of Jowett's *The Works of Plato,* 94; *The Ring and the Book,* 4; use in *The Princess Casamassima,* 91, 94
Review copies, sent to James, 1–2
Roman Empire. *See library list under Gibbon*
Rome. *See library list under Howells; Stendhal*
Romney Marsh. *See library list under Holloway*
Roscoe, William: *Leo the Tenth,* use in *Roderick Hudson,* 76
Rossetti, Dante Gabriel. *See library list under Rossetti, W. M.*
Rousseau, Jean-Jacques. *See library list under Morley*
Ruskin, John. *See library list under Cook; Harrison*
Rye (Sussex): bookshops in, 5. *See also library list under Holloway; Patmore*

Saint-Germain, M. J. T. de, use in *The Princess Casamassima,* 79
Saint-Victor, Paul de, 3. *See also library list under Delzant*
Sainte-Beuve, Charles-Augustin, 76
Sand, George, 3; *La Dernière Aldini,* analogue, in "Travelling Companions," 76. *See also library list under Karénine*
Savonarola, Girolamo. *See library list under Villari*

Schiller, Friedrich: use in "The Death of the Lion," 84
Scott, Sir Walter: use in *The Princess Casamassima,* 80
Scribners: James to, on New York Edition, 94
Selwyn, George. *See library list under Jesse*
Sex: in British fiction, James's criticism of, 82
Shakespeare, William: Eversley edition, 5. *See also library list under Brandes; Daudet, L.; Gosse; Halliwell-Phillips; Hazlitt; Kemble; Lee; Webb*
Shaw, George Bernard, 69. *See also library list under Chesterton*
Shelley, Percy Bysshe, 85; "Ode on Dejection Near Naples," use in "The Sweetheart of M. Briseux," 78. *See also library list under Dowden; Hogg; Medwin*
Sheridan, Richard Brinsley. *See library list under Rae*
Sidney, Sir Philip. *See library list under Symonds*
Sismondi, Jean-Charles-Léonard Simonde de: *Italian Republics,* use in *Roderick Hudson,* 76
Sixte-Quint. See library list under Hubner
Smith, Madeleine. *See library list under Irvine*
Stendhal: *La Chartreuse de Parme,* use in "A Most Extraordinary Case," 76; use in "At Isella," 76; use in "Travelling Companions," 76. *See also library list under Paton; Rod*
Stephan, Leslie. *See library list under Maitland*
Stevenson, Robert Louis: autograph copies of works, 2. *See also library list under Gosse; Henley; Osbourne*
Stewart, Mrs. Duncan, 84
Stratford on Avon. *See library list under Howells*
Stuart, Mary, Queen of Scotland. *See library list under Lang*
Surrey. *See library list under Allen; Cobbett*
Sussex. *See library list under Allen; Patmore; Brickwall, See library list under Trewen*
Swift, Jonathan. *See library list under Collins; Craik*
Swinburne, Algernon. *See library list under Gosse*
Switzerland. *See library list under Symonds*
Symonds, John Addington: use in "The Author of 'Beltraffio,'" 4. *See also library list under Brown*